THE MAKINGS OF A POWERFUL BITCH

THE MAKINGS OF A POWERFUL BITCH

A Woman's Guide to Embracing
Change and Finding Peace and Purpose

SHAWNA OLIVER

ISBN:
E book 979-8-9863247-0-8
Print 979-8-9863247-1-5

Published by Shawna Oliver
www.shawnaoliver.com
Designed by Mary Ann Smith.
Editing by Julia Watson and Yna Davis.
Uploading by Self-Publishing Services
selfpublishingservices.com

To all my wonderful and supportive friends and family, but, above all, to my husband, RDO. When I falter, feel weak, and want to quit, your words of encouragement help replenish my power.

To the many Powerful Bitch publishing experts who helped me take my jumbled words and ideas and turn them into this object of permanence with a soul.

Last but not least, to my clients. Your decision to trust me with your vulnerabilities and dreams will always be viewed as a sacred gift. I continue to learn from you daily.

CONTENTS

INTRODUCTION

Stuckville, USA

You wake up.

You start your day already feeling tired, thinking about all the things you need to manage today—or tomorrow, or later this week—to ensure nothing goes wrong. Because boy, could they. Your belly turns as you mentally prepare your day's to-do list and remember the six different ways that tension and problems at work could boil over, not to mention the potential fallout you have to look forward to after you confront your significant other about the incredibly frustrating thing he did over the weekend.

But hey! You're on top of things. Like most women, you feel you've earned a black belt in multitasking, and if there's one thing you're great at, it's watching out for potential fires—and, if needed, damage control.

On top of all of that—and the ten thousand other things you juggle every day—you have goals you've been trying to reach: To lose weight, get more exercise, or take creative time for yourself. To improve your relationship or change relationships altogether, finally kicking your unsupportive partner to the curb and meeting someone who wants to cheer on your dream-chasing. To get the promotion you know you deserve, after the last one went to someone less experienced and less qualified than you.

It's not like you haven't tried to improve the direction of your life. Heck, you've tried your hand at a million and one different programs and methods to reach that place of happiness that you see daily on your social media feed, that place where *other* people seem to live. You've spent countless hours putting thought and effort into what you need to do to reach a more balanced and positive state, a place where you wake up in the morning actually looking forward to the day after a good night's sleep instead of waking up exhausted after tossing and turning with thoughts of worry running rampant in your head. You're certain that once you find the right program or plan of action, you'll finally experience a lot less stress and a lot more fulfilment.

Only . . . no matter what you do or how much you achieve, this place of contentment seems to stay three steps ahead of you, a constantly moving target. You hate to admit it, even to yourself, but at this point, you've tried and failed so many times that, honestly, it's hard to muster the energy you need to get up and try again.

And it's not like you're an unintelligent woman. You know your stuff. You've done the research. I bet you could tell me exactly how exercise helps manage your stress, how many calories are in the muffin you're about to eat, and how your lack of sleep is messing with both your productivity and your mood, making an already-challenging life seem even tougher.

So why is it that every time you try to make changes in your life to make things better, you either start and stop or you never quite manage to begin in the first place?

I won't tell you the solution is simple because it's not. Okay, maybe it's a *little* simple. More importantly, it's attainable. I know because my clients and I have experienced fundamental and remarkable transformations, ones that had previously eluded us for decades.

It sounds cheesy as hell, I know, but please bear with me. We found our inner power, which leads to a lot more peace and—dare I say—happiness.

And how did we pull this off, you ask?

We owned our shit. We got to really know ourselves, warts and all. We embraced truly living in the moment. We learned to understand and love all the inner parts of ourselves and to treat them with the respect they need so that we can support the best performance from each of them.

In short, dear reader, we—each of us—became our very best Powerful Bitch selves. And I'm going to teach you how to do that too.

Zen and the Art of Bitch Mastery

So, what is a Powerful Bitch?

A Powerful Bitch doesn't wake up every day hoping to finally catch confidence, peace, or happiness. She doesn't have to—because after doing the inner work found in this book, she now lives as the practicing embodiment of each of those things. She no longer gets distracted by the useless messages in her head, the what-ifs, oh-craps, do-betters, and well-what-abouts. She has learned that being powerful means capturing opportunities for growth and change but also gaining a quiet certainty in her capacity to handle life's less enjoyable companions: stress, heartbreak, and regret, to name a few.

One thing a Powerful Bitch is *not* is someone who never gets stressed out. Sorry, that's still going to happen sometimes. But a Powerful Bitch *does* know how to listen to her body for signals that a stress response is starting up. And she knows exactly what self-soothing tools she has at her disposal to counteract stress and get herself back into the state of calm needed to fully understand what's really happening, allowing her to respond effectively, meeting core needs.

A Powerful Bitch values all aspects of self-care and takes time to prioritize it—because she knows her main job in life is not to care for others above herself at all times—and when she wants and needs to be there for the people she loves, she will be at her best to do so. This strong foundation of self-care allows her to more boldly say yes to life's opportunities and richness.

Lastly, a Powerful Bitch has two incredibly important things: self-awareness and mindful self-compassion. She understands her own strengths and flaws, and she has learned to love herself exactly as she is, even as she strives for improvement. She has even begun to laugh at herself and to admit when she makes mistakes, without it becoming a source of panic or pain. (I solemnly swear this is possible, and I say that as a dyed-in-the-wool lifelong perfectionist.)

Bottom line: A Powerful Bitch knows what she actually wants versus only seeing what she doesn't want. She understands that sometimes she feels undeserving of all that goodness, but also knows this is just part of the process of becoming something more than she is today. She has developed the ability to be in the present moment and respect her own needs in life's magical unfolding. She knows how to embrace the joy of being with the people around her without always trying to perform to some ambiguous impossibly high standard.

This is what I'm trying to tell you, in a nutshell. Living with self-love and peace isn't three steps ahead of where you're sitting right now. It's not on the other side of any goal, or exclusive to people you only keep in touch with via Facebook or Instagram these days.

The life you want is sitting right next to you, waving its hand invisibly in front of your face, trying to get your attention. You're just too busy worrying about everything else going on to see it.

Where is it?

It's the excitement in your kid's voice as they try to tell you about the cool thing that happened at school today. It's in the colors of the sunset while you're driving home from work. It's the hopeful, beautiful story your friend tells you, the one that you could actually be listening to and getting something wonderful out of if only you weren't focused on the niggling worry you've been chewing on all day like a dog with a bone. It's in the strength of your legs and the feel of the rain as you go for a run.

Peace and happiness are already present in your days, and you don't even know it. But we're gonna change that, you and I.

Your Guide to Peace, Purpose, and Bitch-Wrangling

So, you might be wondering right about here who this crazy lady is who's telling you that the answer to all your problems is to embrace your inner bitch. Reader, you're not alone. My clients ask themselves this too. But by the time they come through my door, they—like you—have tried so many fad diets and trendy exercise regimens, joined so many dating apps, changed jobs so many times, and read so many self-help books that they don't even know where to begin anymore. Not only that, but they're sick and tired of trying.

You see, it's not just that they're confused and hurting—they're angry with themselves for hurting. I've been there too, struggling silently, putting on a happy face to keep from bothering anyone with my messy emotions. Feeling lonely, even when surrounded by others. Squashing dreams out of fear of failure—or worse, of success.

Many of us are living similarly frustrating experiences, with no proper guide on how to reset our lives back to the state of joy and optimism we once held, long ago. That is why I wrote this book, to offer you the guide I wish I'd had back when I needed it.

I searched for a guide like this for years. In the end, my answers were not found in a single book but began with an interview for a job I didn't get, resulting in a life-changing introduction to my current career. This journey led me to train to become a certified health and wellness coach in 2012. It was in this training that I began to learn the core fundamentals needed to start the process of adopting different ways of *being*. It's funny—I can say that now in hindsight, but I was . . . let's say resistant to much of what I was being shown in the beginning. I mean, how dare my instructors tell me that, to be a good coach, I first had to do the things I would go on to teach my clients to do, that I had to practice mindful awareness, being present, and sitting with my own positive *and* negative emotions? What was the point of wasting my valuable time on navel-gazing and examining all that baggage? No way was I going to do that. All of that crap was far better left in the box I'd packed it all into and shoved into a distant corner of my mind. I was sure all I needed was to be the best learner; then I would know everything I needed to and be able to help people fix their problems. Wrong!

Despite my obstinance, my instructors persisted. And then they just had to bring science into it. Understand, reader, that in my first career, I was a registered nurse for twenty-five years. And these experts had *the nerve* to bring in things like functional MRI brain scan imagery and scientific journal research showing that all this positive psychology, mindfulness, self-compassion, and mindset change stuff *really worked?!*

Ugh.

I remember the moment clearly when I realized I was going to have to do all the work on myself that I'd been so adamantly opposed to. I actually tossed a stack of books (my assigned reading for class, naturally) clear across the coffee table. They slid to the floor, landing with a solid thump. "Fuck," I said to myself. "I'm going to have to meditate."

This was the beginning of my difficult years of radical, transformational change, and I am happy to say I came out the other side with newfound grace and peace. My particular lifelong poison is perfectionism. It's something I have struggled with all my life, and it kept me focused on making sure I didn't do anything "wrong" or less than "perfect" every moment of every day. I can see now that I had thoroughly convinced myself that if everything looked just so on the outside, then no one would be able to tell how painful and messy things were on the inside.

So what changed for me? I was still working as a nurse at the time, and, with the slow adoption of the practices in this book, I found myself able to make gains in change. While at work, I began to do simple things like homing in on what patients were really saying to me. During conversations, instead of focusing on all the things I had to do (and do just right) for the rest of the day, I started really listening to the people I was there with in the moment. I learned to focus on making sure I heard what each patient's number one priority was, on making sure *they knew* I'd heard it, and then on delivering that one most important thing.

The change this made in my day-to-day work life was immediately noticeable. My patient interactions became deeper, and patients verbalized being understood and feeling safer when in my care. That's what happens when someone in need feels truly heard and seen: they relax and can heal faster. What's more, *I* felt different. Calmer. More able to handle daily stresses and challenges. More confident and hopeful. This newfound energy and awareness was also adopted in my personal life, exponentially improving my relationships with my kids, my husband, and my friends. I was finally able to embrace the pos-sibility that I was enough, just as I was—and ironically, to the people who really loved me, it had always been so.

Today, I'm a board-certified health and wellness coach. I've enjoyed a solo practice since January 2018 and have helped countless women like you reconnect to a purpose and passion for living. I was among the first class of graduates to be certified through the National Board for Health and Wellness Coaching, a nonprofit agency created to set standards for the profession of health coaching with validated criteria for education and training. Their examinations were created in collaboration with the National Board of Medical Examiners (the board that licenses medical doctors in the US). I'm also certified through Wellcoaches, which is affiliated with the American College of Lifestyle Medicine and the American College of Sports Medicine. I have been published by Thrive Global, written for a nonprofit book for COVID relief funds, and been featured as an expert on local TV and print news, as well as on several radio and podcast episodes. On the personal front, I've been married to my husband, Roger, for twenty-eight years and have co-parented four sons, two stepsons followed by two biological sons. (Yep, all boys. My place in heaven is assured.)

Through the blessing of my coaching practice, I have been able to gain the hands-on evidence needed to demonstrate that the tools I learned to use to help myself can offer just as much healing for women struggling similarly. I remain certain that women don't need more of those catchy life-hack-type tips and suggestions, they need real tools and guides on how to create their own personal formulas for peace and purpose. Women need to be understood, and, most importantly, we need to *understand ourselves*. As for how we actually use those tools once we learn them? That's up to each of us individually because we all have our own rich stories of life lessons and possess unique and sacred hopes and wishes.

And these tools, once you have them in your arsenal and up your sleeve? Dang. Those are the makings of a Powerful Bitch.

How to Use This Book

I've organized the information in this book so that each chapter tackles a key topic directly related to embracing change and finding peace and purpose.

Here's a quick rundown of what's in store.

Chapter One: Meet Your Three Inner Bitches. Here I'll introduce you to Survival Bitch, Charge Bitch, and Repetitive Bitch—the Inner Bitches who already live and work inside of you. What? You didn't think Powerful Bitch was the only bitch in this story, did you? Familiarizing yourself with what each one of them is designed to handle will help you to better understand how your mind and body work so that, when you're ready to implement big changes in your life, you know what you've got to work with starting out.

Chapter Two: Priming Your Power: Self-Care for Bitches. It's all but impossible to transform into the best possible version of yourself if you're not taking good care of who you are right now. Here we'll cover crucial self-care basics required to keep Charge Bitch on her A game.

Chapter Three: Managing Stress, or How to Avoid "Charge Bitch Has Left the Building!" The inability to manage and cope with stress is incredibly common, and out-of-control stress symptoms are one of the biggest barriers preventing long-term positive change in our lives—sometimes before we even really get started. Here you'll learn the ins and outs of how to (and how not to) deal with stress.

Chapter Four: Mindfulness: The Bird's-Eye View of Inner Bitch Actions. Time and time again, my clients and I find that the number one key to finding peace and purpose in life is being able to take a step back from what we're thinking and feeling to pause and appreciate the possibility of another perspective, instead of getting caught up in old behaviors, patterns, and the stories we tell ourselves. Here we'll look at how to use mindfulness practices to gain the insight needed to get things headed in the right direction.

Chapter Five: Self-Compassion: Healing Survival Bitch. Another place where we women tend to get stuck when trying to make positive changes in our lives is being so self-critical and unkind to ourselves that we can't channel the belief and energy needed to change in the first place. Here you'll learn what it means to be truly self-compassionate and how these practices actually help foster change.

Chapter Six: Hijack Your Own Habits: How to Rewire Repetitive Bitch for Winning. All right, here's where we really get cracking with creating change. In this chapter, I'll show you how to get Repetitive Bitch and her coconspirator Bitches to work *for* you instead of against you when you're trying to change your habits to change your life.

Chapter Seven: How to Embrace Change like a Powerful Bitch. Up to this point in the book, I'll have been teaching you a variety of skills and tools you can use to become your best Powerful Bitch self. Here, we'll add some fine-tuning and best practices for creating and sticking with the positive changes you're making.

Chapter Eight: The Powerful Bitch Realized. Finally, I'll offer my vision of what's next for you as you prepare for the personal transformation you've been looking to create. I'll also provide some resources you can use as you take your first steps on this journey.

Even if some chapters jump out at you more than others up front, I recommend reading this book from beginning to end the first time through. It's been structured so that the ideas you learn in the first few chapters form the foundation needed to use each new tool or skill that's shared further on.

The Road Ahead

Here's a moment of brutal vulnerability for you: The thought of someone other than my husband reading this book is scary for me, not just because I am being my true and authentic (i.e., highly imperfect) self in it, but because it is written in glaring opposition to all the behaviors, thoughts, and habits that I was certain kept me safe for years and years of my life. That's the "before" Shawna, seen through present-day Shawna's compassionate lens.

I used to pretend to have it all together, acting like I knew all the correct answers and feigning happiness, all while being so damn serious and busy in my own head that I missed the full richness of life's tapestry as it continued to unfold right in front of me.

"Before" Shawna clearly did not have all of her shit together. Even so, she got me here, where I am today, and I have to honor her for that. Loving myself so that I can have more peace means recognizing that my missteps, mistakes, and struggles ultimately honed me into someone with more humility, gratitude, and compassion for others.

Believe it or not, this is one of the most important keys to becoming a Powerful Bitch. The journey isn't always graceful and pretty, and we're not always at our best. But who is?

That's right. Say it with me: *nobody*.

Nobody is always at their best. The trick is to know yourself well enough to be able to refocus and see things clearly, even in the middle of a very bumpy section of road. You can handle the little bit of discomfort that comes with growth and change. I have faith in you. You have the capacity to manage that. The benefits of gaining more peace and purpose are immeasurable. Once you have the tools within you, they will carry you across many rough stretches in life, as well as on those paths of growth and change.

This book is meant to serve as both your road map and toolbox for that journey, and for all the unexpected stops along the way. Our goal is to get you out of the day-to-day survival mode you've been existing in for far too long.

And when you come out on the other side, you'll find that you have a newfound sense of freedom—freedom to enjoy your life, to laugh, to *play*. Suddenly, every day is a chance to do kind things for others because you genuinely *want* to, not because you fear not being needed or worry about being judged for what you didn't do.

When you own who you are and step into the shoes of your very best Powerful Bitch self, days aren't just something to get through anymore. They're something to genuinely look forward to. Each and every one is a chance to express yourself as an authentic human being, to be seen and appreciated— including and *especially* by yourself—for who you really are.

That is the journey we're on together, you and me. What do you say we take the first step and be on our way?

First up, before you can become the Powerful Bitch you were always meant to be, it's time to get to know the Bitches who live and work inside you already. And you may be asking, why does this Shawna person insist on us calling parts of ourselves *bitches*, anyway? We'll cover all of this in chapter 1, where you'll meet the three powerful internal drives in every woman that I like to refer to as your Three Inner Bitches.

In this next chapter, we'll explore what each of the Three Inner Bitches represents in our day-to-day ability to function. We'll also learn some of the inspirational neuroscience that informed the character creation of these Inner Bitches. Learning these basics will help explain how our habits and survival instincts inform our choices and how we can learn to take better care of ourselves and make smarter decisions, even when times are tough.

Well, what are you waiting for? Let's get started.

CHAPTER ONE

MEET YOUR THREE INNER BITCHES

> "Do you ever look at someone and wonder,
> 'What is going on inside their head?'"
> — Joy from the movie *Inside Out*

The Three Inner Bitches: A New Take on Neuroscience

The fact that you picked up this book tells me that there's something in your life you want to alter or improve upon. Something you've not had a lot of luck with so far—some change you'd like to make in your career, your personal life, or both. You've probably tried more than a few things to achieve your goals by now, but nothing seems to stick. Or maybe you can't bring yourself to get started on the thing you think you need to do to solve your problems in the first place.

The reality is that change is hard. It's not as simple as making a decision and doing the thing—otherwise, we'd all be walking, talking role models of human perfection. What I see play out from my coaching chair is that most of us are just striving to live out the potential we know we have within us and truly enjoy our lives.

You see, you will never convince me that people don't go to the gym if they are capable because "they are lazy" or that they don't quit smoking because "they have no interest." Nor do people choose not to end shitty relationships because "they enjoy being unhappy." Each of us has very distinct reasons for not acting in ways that would, by all appearances, result in us living healthier and happier lives. I'm going to spend the rest of our time together in this book showing you that, while change is hard, it is doable, with the right set of tools and understanding.

Enter the Three Inner Bitches, the parts of us that we'll be using to personify the basic drives that we use every day to navigate our world and *get things done*. Understanding these ladies and their idiosyncrasies allows for real and permanent change because fully knowing and loving them all gives rise to the creation of your most Powerful Bitch self. And understand, I'm not talking about a temporary Band-Aid to fix a problem, like a fad diet or a viral TikTok exercise craze that you try for a week and then quit. Women who learn to grow into and embrace their Powerful Bitch selves not only change what they do but how they think and how they react spontaneously to everyday life situations and choices. With awareness, internal motivation, and intentional action, they eventually find themselves going through life responding in surprising new ways, completely contrary to how they may have acted in the past.

Before we go further, please allow me to add a small but vital sidenote. Throughout this book, I am assuming that your basic life necessities are met and that you are—for the most part—mentally well. Considering the hierarchy of needs, though, if you do not have security in the vital areas of food, shelter, and safety, it is nearly impossible to begin striving for the best version of yourself. If you are suffering from addiction or mental health issues, please seek out the best resources available to you for assistance in first tackling these challenges. Your primary care physician is a good place to start and can guide you with referrals to other professionals or local agencies that specialize in options best suited to your needs.

In this chapter, you'll meet your Three Inner Bitches and begin to understand how each plays a unique and important role in your ability to do just about anything. But first, we'll cover just enough basic neuroscience to help you understand the scientific underpinnings and key concepts that you need to put *your* Three Bitches to work for you so that you can ultimately become your version of a Powerful Bitch.

Inner Bitch Neuroscience 101

Now, I know you are eager to get this show on the road and meet your Inner Bitches. They are waiting just around the corner. I promise! Before we get to them, though, I first want to go over those neuroscience concepts I mentioned to prime you for maximum understanding of how each Inner Bitch behaves within you and allows you to function—you know, this whole adulting thing that we are expected to do day in and day out.

Now, let me preface this by saying that obviously I am not a neuroscience specialist! So, while I can't give you exact specifics as to the delicate intricacies of the mind and its precise biological underpinnings—the mysteries of how we think, feel, and act represent areas that we're learning more about literally every day—what I can do is arm you with some useful basics to serve as a foundation for everything that's coming next. I have gathered a respectable amount of information on this topic. And what I've found is that knowing a little about this stuff has proven to be effective for my clients, time and time again.

The way I describe the various areas and functions of the brain I'll be referencing in this book is simplified and put in laywoman's terms for ease of use. Understanding how your brain works (even just the highlights) offers ideas you can actually imagine and use to make changes that get your mind working *for* you instead of against you. That's really what this entire book is about. At the end of the day, our Inner Bitches are constructs we're going to use to better understand all aspects of ourselves and how to be Powerful Bitches by potentiating their combined power.

In that spirit, below are some terms and concepts I think you'll find helpful as we go along.

Neurons are cells and are the basic working units of the brain. They are core components of the brain, spinal cord, and peripheral nerves, but throughout this book, when I refer to neurons, know that for our purposes here, I am referring specifically to the ones in your brain (other than in one small section in chapter 2 on gut health).

Neurotransmitters are chemical substances that neurons use to transmit information. They transmit electrical impulses from one neuron to another, like messengers.

Neurogenesis is the process by which new neurons are formed in the brain. This is a crucial process that happens before we're born but can continue throughout the entire human lifespan.

Neuroplasticity is the ability of the brain to undergo physiological or structural changes, especially in response to learning, experience, or injury. The physical neural networks in some parts of our brains are capable of being altered. It was long assumed that adult brains could not grow and change. Scientists now understand that our brains are more pliable than previously thought, and many areas can adapt, grow, and change based on what we expose them to and what we do with them habitually.

Which brings us to *habits*. A habit is a repeatedly performed behavior or pattern of thinking that results in physically and permanently wiring neural connections in the lower part of your brain, the basal ganglia. Once set, habits are easily and almost effortlessly followed, but can be challenging to change.

To summarize, all these terms add up to your powerful ability to use intention to do or think something new, to create a new brain pattern, to pause, pay full attention, hold, and repeat to permanently change your mind—and therefore yourself—in all senses of the word.

Okay, now that we're past your new vocabulary words, we're almost to the really good stuff. But while we're on the subject of how words are used, there's one more thing on the agenda.

A Word from Our Sponsors

Let's get one more thing out of the way here about terminology, because I know some of you have been thinking, "Why do I have to refer to parts of who I am as *bitches*?"

Yes, *bitch* can be such a strange word for us as women. In the past, it was mainly used as a derogatory term, and it still is in some cases. But like many such words, it has been reclaimed by current generations. Over time, the word *bitch* has changed and morphed into more of a catchall with a variety of uses, including as a loving greeting or name.

Initially, I had some hesitation in naming our inner players *bitches*. But then I thought about how my close friends and I refer to each other in this way, and how playful and loving a term it can be—how *seen* it can make us feel, and what a sense of belonging it brings. We aren't just bitches. We're *each other's* bitches.

I want you to think of your Inner Bitches like this—like sisters or old friends who live inside of you, who are a part of you. As I hope to demonstrate going forward, each one of these Inner Bitches possesses uniquely remarkable characteristics, talents, and abilities that allow us to be complete and wonderful beings.

Speaking of which, it's time to talk about those powers. That's right: it's time for some long-awaited introductions.

Meet Your Three Inner Bitches

I've seen it time and time again with my clients: getting to know your Three Inner Bitches is irrefutably life-changing. Why is that? Because knowledge *used with intention* is power. Understanding the science of how our brains work means that instead of blindly going through our days frustrated and not understanding why we do the things we do, we grant ourselves the insight needed to forgive our human failings and limitations and to take specific action toward positive change. Coming to know these parts of ourselves via the constructs of the Three Inner Bitches makes that life-changing understanding more tangible, relatable, and hopefully funny.

Each of these Three Bitches who live inside of us all has her own strengths and weaknesses. Each works best for some situations and less so for others. The key, like in all inner work, is having the self-compassion to love them all equally, no matter their fallacies. Once you do this, you can decide much more easily which one has the most appropriate strengths for any given challenge that pops up for you and respond accordingly.

As described below, each of the Three Inner Bitches *roughly* represents her associated area of the brain. Neuroscience is complicated, and we're trying to keep things fairly simple for our purposes here. With that in mind, we're going to get a little creative with how to apply neuroscience concepts, because I want you to be able to see yourself in this somewhat ridiculous but beautiful cast of characters.

Meet Survival Bitch, aka Your Limbic Center

Survival Bitch is someone each of us was born with. She has been there literally from Day One. And unless you suffer a catastrophic brain injury or have just emptied several bottles of wine into your face hole, she fights to stay front and center until the day you die.

Survival Bitch is *always* present, and she isn't afraid to create a little mayhem if that's what's required to ensure that you are A) still breathing and B) getting your needs met. After all, you staying alive is her prime directive, modus operandi, and raison d'être. She is both your ever-present inner hall monitor and your wine aunt. One minute she's watching for Freddy Krueger at the grocery store and assessing exit routes, and the next she's seeking out your favorite flavor of ice cream with extra chocolate pieces. "Oooh," she coos. "Is that a wine sale?!" Yes, Survival Bitch. Yes, it is. Her interests range from a simple taste of sugar as a reward for all the hard work of living to the complex human needs of learning and attachment.

Survival Bitch is strength, speed, and persistence. She sends continual messages to the other areas of your brain and body, especially ones that concern safety or rewards. At times, her constant presence can be annoying, but nonetheless, she is a vital undercurrent of your day-to-day life.

What's more, Survival Bitch is also a neurochemical, all-hands-on-deck shitstorm if you ever need to do something like jump out of the way of oncoming traffic. She can process sensory information with lightning speed and tells you to jump in the ditch, not think, "Hey that's a remodeled Mustang GT500" as a car comes careening toward you. She is all your senses plus the vast tentacles of hormonal and biochemical responses that have control over your heart rate, blood pressure, glucose level, and even your hormone-driven Oreo-eating binges. She can be temperamental, but also has within herself the warm tingly sensations of *big love*.

You can often notice what Survival Bitch is telling you if you pay attention to how your body feels below your neck. There might be an all-over ache of loneliness, or butterflies in your stomach when you're excited, or a tightness in your chest from an argument with your partner. All of this is Survival Bitch's territory. She can direct the signals within your nervous system to "Slow down! . . . No, just kidding, speed up!" with the use of hormones and brain chemicals.

Survival Bitch is focused on what's happening *right now*, and she often prefers comfort over the lack of it because back in primitive times comfort was a rarity. She is happy luxuriating in a warm bath, receiving a pedi, or maybe even snuggling under a blanket with a bowl of popcorn while she binge-watches whatever she can find on Hulu. She can be thanked for your racing heart or sweaty palms when you go on a first date or get into yet another argument with your coworker about their cloying perfume in your shared cubicle.

Survival Bitch runs the show a lot more than we give her credit for. She has and *is* gut feelings, that ol' Spidey-Sense thing that tells you the guy on the phone is not really from Publishers Clearing House, no matter the song he sings. If something hurts physically or mentally, she makes damn sure that info is given priority storage space in long-term memory, so you know how to respond rapidly and escape that particular mess in the future.

While you were born with many of Survival Bitch's powers, life added layers to her ideas and beliefs, and therefore to her automatic reactions. Her survival needs are much deeper than basic food and shelter. In order to achieve and maintain true security, she needs autonomy, acceptance, competency, and a deep-rooted sense of belonging.

Meet Charge Bitch, aka Your Prefrontal Cortex

During my nursing career, I worked many years on the night shift, side by side with anywhere from five to eight other rock-star nurses. We all had different personalities, but many of us cultivated strong wills and the tough attitude needed to manage the fast pace and inherent chaos found in a hospital setting. While we all had passionate, intelligent energy, assignments had to be divvied up: someone had to lead crisis management, plan breaks, hold her cool, and be the spokesperson to supervisors. This role was lovingly known as the "Charge Bitch."

Guess what? You have one of those too, better known as your prefrontal cortex. She is a management-level genius. Without her playing her part, you wouldn't have been able to add to your *Britannica* series-sized volumes of knowledge, year after freakin' brilliant year. She can juggle all that information in real time to plan, organize, and complete high-level, complex tasks. She can compute difficult math problems and chemical equations, if she has been given the opportunity to learn how.

Charge Bitch loves *language*. I cannot emphasize this enough. She loves to deal in words! She possesses fabulous short-term working memory but makes choices considering her long-term future. The part of you that is concerned about 401(k) s and shit? Yeah, that's Charge Bitch. She's an upstanding member of society.

This is because Charge Bitch understands, in her analytical, executive-decision-making noggin, what is best for you. She is the voice speaking when my clients ask, "Why do I always . . . ?" or, "Why can't I seem to . . . ?" Charge Bitch sees beyond the now. She creatively imagines and maps out future goals and wishes. She plans meals and trips, arranges schedules in multiples, and can build a smooth-running family machine and/or a Fortune 500 company.

Unfortunately, while the power of imagination can be used for strategizing and planning, it can also have its downsides, as in the case of chronic worry and its triggering anxiety. Charge Bitch can also work with belief systems (conscious or subconscious) that are not always helpful and can take things a little too ("Blame me. It must be my fault . . .") personally. We'll address this more soon.

If she has the energy, Charge Bitch can regulate your behavior and even manage and override the other Inner Bitches' responses. When she's in charge, you know it. She can shut down your habit of scrolling social media at work to get that project done. You use her to not yell at your boss or your kids. She keeps you out of jail. She makes an immeasurable number of decisions every hour of every day. She follows deadlines. When you are rested and her energy has not been drained by stress, she makes the impossible possible.

We like to believe we can command Charge Bitch's performance any time, but that is easier said than done. May I present evidence by way of Exhibit 1: the salad and salmon dinner plans you skipped last night in favor of feasting on wine and whoopie pies over the kitchen island? Charge Bitch can't do her best work on sugar alone. Another source of kryptonite for Charge Bitch is her tendency to get stuck in what is commonly known as "analysis paralysis," a place where decision-making is postponed while she contemplates a *War and Peace*-sized pros and cons list. This can happen because, even with all the common-sense pros, something feels absolutely wrong in the pit of Survival Bitch's stomach.

Additionally, because she requires quite a high level of energy to move mountains, Charge Bitch's output is not limitless. After she focuses fully for ninety minutes or so, her performance powers start to drain. Push her too far without breaks and food refuels, and her quality of work can become lower-rated than a preteen boy's hygiene practices.

She can sometimes appear clinical and cold. If she were fully in charge, you might not be able to love as big, cry as hard, fully embrace the sensations of a warm hug, bask in the smell of your child's hair, or stare at the clouds in the sky for an hour.

When it comes to body sensations, you notice Charge Bitch's work and relate to her best in the areas above your neck. When she is in charge, decision-making is effortless, and your mind is clear and functioning well. She can direct you to bypass your kids' cold leftover fries, and she is on board to easily ace the mandatory training exam at work.

Meet Repetitive Bitch, aka Your Habit Center

This is the part of you that watches *Good Morning America* every day over two cups of coffee. She puts her pants on left leg first. Repetitive Bitch, or your habit center, is you on autopilot, performing everyday tasks and running the bleepin' show without having to use a lot of brain power. She is your Vanna White, turning those letters for thirty-nine-plus years in a semi-conscious state. A habitual efficiency machine, Repetitive Bitch is a conveyor belt of kids' breakfasts, packed lunches, drives to work, and tasks repeated in the same daily order: emails, LinkedIn, phone messages, and . . . ooh, break time.

Many of Repetitive Bitch's hardwired actions were born out of necessity, like finding the most efficient way to tie your shoes and button your coat. But while she is your habitual response to physical routines, she also responds in a routine manner to mental and emotional situations. That's not always a good thing, and clients often seek my help to address concerns with her.

So, how did Repetitive Bitch develop? I alluded to her origins in my earlier description of habits. The first time we perform a novel action, it requires Charge Bitch's energy, effort, working memory, concentration, and perhaps some willpower. However, once we *complete* that new action, or think a group of newly learned thoughts, that action or thought pattern is categorized in our minds and bodies. If the thinking pattern or behavior resulted in positive neu-rotransmitter production from a "win," offered a sense of safety or relief, or provided a human connection or bonding hormones, then our brains label it as positive and say, "Well done! Let's try to repeat that again, shall we?" Survival Bitch tells Charge Bitch, "Let's both remember exactly how this felt and what actions and/or circumstances made it happen and do it again if the opportunity arises, okay?" Conversely, if the brain has categorized that thought pattern or behavior as a negative experience, like one that results in pain of the physical or mental variety? Then Survival Bitch says, "Ugh. Let's flag that mess. And if anything like that ever comes up again, stay the hell away from it!" Avoid but-ton installed.

And you do or do not do, again and again. And one more time, again. With greater repetition of that thought or behavior and the learning of a routine, thinking and decision-making needs decrease until they are essentially no longer required. As Repetitive Bitch repeats, Charge Bitch is simply losing her dominant role. The response habituates and happens rapidly without much notice or attention.

Habits, those aforementioned linked clusters of brain cells permanent-ly encoded into the lower part of the brain, are where Repetitive Bitch lives. She performs a habit sequence seamlessly and without much awareness as soon as she receives a signal from Survival Bitch's senses that a situation looks, feels, smells, or sounds like something she has encountered in the past. This is commonly called the habit "cue." The cue to a repetitive action or thought is received and processed unbelievably quickly and easily, *even* if what once seemed like a good survival strategy or a well-deserved reward as far as the Inner Bitches are concerned has now become a problem.

Like all the Bitches, Repetitive Bitch is often helpful, but she is also perniciously stubborn with her sticky rituals and routines. She insists on continually playing them out, even though Charge Bitch has sat her down and had many serious, logical conversations with her, explaining that this or that particular shit is just no longer helpful.

Repetitive Bitch constantly picks up physiological or mental cues from your environment, your internal bodily sensations, or even your thinking patterns and responds automatically. A sight, smell, place, or thought sets Repetitive Bitch scurrying toward that particular sensory information's automatic response, oftentimes before Charge Bitch has even had a chance to give her input. Too late—Repetitive Bitch is off to the races!

How the Inner Bitches Work—or Don't Work—Together

As you might imagine, each Inner Bitch has a distinctive approach to any given situation. For instance, in the nursing world, Charge Bitch smiles at your supervisor and reports on patients while Repetitive Bitch sets up her one thousandth IV. Survival Bitch, still peeved from her last employee review, gives your boss the finger the moment she turns her back.

Charge Bitch plans a healthy dinner, but Survival Bitch says, "Screw that! I deserve a treat because I am tired and my head hurts." Repetitive Bitch blindly walks to the fridge while talking on the phone to her bestie about her boss being an ass and makes a grab for the wine and cheese.

Survival Bitch feels your spouse's unexpected and annoying pat on the bum while you are doing the dishes in peace. She's the one who jumps and shrieks, and then Charge Bitch tells the internal story that begins with "What a jerk!" and starts to strategize a comeuppance for "that neanderthal."

Those examples are snapshots of three everyday moments and descriptions of how our Inner Bitches play into our responses, behaviors, and thoughts. Now, here is where things start to get messy, because as humans we are obviously beautiful but mercurial and complex beings, so the details of how any of these scenarios might play out are as varied as we are as people. In other versions of the nursing shift scenario, someone else's Charge Bitch may have underestimated that her Survival Bitch tends to be complacent and accommodating and often takes on extra work from anyone and everyone. Another nurse may be bored unless she uses her Charge Bitch to the max, so she always volunteers for the most complex cases. Yet another person's Survival Bitch might only feel safe when she is in control, so she argues about patient assignments with her supervisor right up until the shift ends.

Now, where many of us go wrong when we try to make positive changes in our lives is we try to accomplish this by pushing and cajoling ourselves instead of understanding our Inner Bitches' needs, wants, and fears. Once you get to know them and are able to show each of these parts of yourself a little self-compassion as needed, you can learn how to work with them in harmony rather than against them. The trick lies in gaining the self-awareness to be able to notice who's getting a little rambunctious and why when trouble rears its head.

Now that you have a basic grasp on who your Inner Bitches are and what role each plays in your ability to do all the incredible things you do each day, you're primed and ready to learn more about how to get them to work together more effectively. In the next chapter, we're going to learn the important role that self-care plays in creating positive, long-lasting change in our lives. After all, you can't build the new and improved you if the current you isn't getting her needs met.

CHAPTER TWO:

PRIMING YOUR POWER: SELF-CARE FOR BITCHES

"It is a common experience that a problem difficult
at night is resolved in the morning after the
committee of sleep has worked on it."
—John Steinbeck

Shaky Platforms Can't Support Change

Let's say you have been given endless resources to build your dream home, fully tricked out with whatever you want inside of it. The perfect kitchen with an industrial-grade stove if you like to cook. A crafting room with every tool, art supply, and doodad you could ever dream of if that's your thing. Or maybe what you want is a ginormous great room for gathering with friends and family, with one of those plush couch groupings the size of Rhode Island. Whatever it is you're into, this new home is gonna be the perfect pad to enjoy that in.

There's just one catch.

You can only build this house on a plot of land that straddles a massive seismic fault line. There's a big crack running through the plot, *two feet wide*. And what's that over there? Oh, that's the gaping abyss that opened up the other day, which you'd rather not look at or think about. It's right where your bedroom is supposed to go. Sure, there's an earthquake here every few weeks and that crack seems to be getting wider. But it should be fine, right?

. . . Right?

Okay. I hear you. You'd *never* build a house on ground like that. But here's the thing. You, like most people, have almost certainly been trying to build your best self on shaky, unstable ground sprung from your lack of basic daily self-care routines.

Now, when I talk about self-care, I'm not talking pedicures, although, don't get me wrong, they're great. What I'm speaking of is how you treat yourself in all aspects of living, from nutrition, to sleep hygiene, to alone time, relationship discourse, working environments, dream-chasing . . . the whole enchilada.

What do I mean when I say *your platform?* I mean the physiology, chemistry, and structures that make up both your mind and body. I like to highlight the aspects you control, which are reflected in all your daily habits of self-care. These are the behaviors you do to maximize your platform's strength or weaken its foundation. Caring for your platform impacts how you feel and how you think. Both impact your emotions. In turn, your emotions impact your life experience in every way possible. I stress the importance of self-care because a shaky platform will lead to shaky mindsets and halt your progress toward changing your life in its tracks. It can be helpful to begin with remembering that, as human beings, we remain tied to our biological needs and rhythms and thousands of years of genetics. These factors influence how we function and feel—as much as our sleep-deprived, around-the-clock work schedules, fast food, and numbing-away-the-pain current lifestyles try to prove otherwise.

Food, exercise, and sleep routines become vital pieces in the larger scheme of maintaining the beautiful machine that is your body and mind. In my experience, respect and kindness to both are necessary. After all, both are often needed to create the moments that offer peak satisfaction and joy. Both offer the foundational support to create your own form of success. Less-than-optimal platforms just can't hold up grandiose dreams, the kind of dreams that require the endurance and fortitude to push through when challenges naturally arise. The kind of dreams worth fighting for.

The Body-Mind Connection

To begin, I really need you to trust me when I say that the body and the mind are not separate entities. How you treat one affects the other, and vice versa.

The way I like to explain this to my clients is that your body's chemistry is akin to the petri dish your brain cells sit in to grow bacterial thoughts. Now, some bacteria are good and helpful, while other kinds are . . . not. The same goes for the thoughts developing in that petri dish of body chemistry.

If your petri dish is full of cortisol (stress chemicals) and devoid of things like dopamine, serotonin, and oxytocin (positive brain chemicals), your brain becomes fertile ground for worry and overwhelm. When your habits around self-care suffer, so too does the environment of your precious brain.

And this is a two-way street. For example, if the quality of Charge Bitch's thought patterns is consistently negative, it will *literally* change the chemical state and physiology of your being. Alert messages get sent to Survival Bitch's command center, creating a bodily reaction and sensory experiences like pain, fatigue, headaches, temporomandibular joint disorders, muscle tightness in the neck, jaw, upper back, and shoulders, or digestive issues. These and a host of other ailments have long been documented as symptoms of depression, chronic stress, and anxiety.

When your petri dish is full of the good stuff, though, your brain chemistry essentially works like a buffer against stress and worry, increasing your resilience in the face of life's stresses and challenges. This allows you to focus on kicking names and taking—wait. I think I got that backward. You get where I'm going with this.

The good news is that, when you engage in healthy activities, you can chemically tweak your body to be primed for optimal functioning and mood states. This will set the stage to rewire your brain's habits of doing and thinking and make permanent change.

Please note that it is *not* my intent to dismiss mental health disorders here. As I mentioned in chapter 1, if you're currently dealing with a mental health crisis, it's time to focus first on getting yourself to a better, stronger place, rather than focusing on trying to make major life changes right now. This book is about taking things to the next level for those of us lucky enough to only need the tools and strategies to potentiate what we currently are blessed to possess.

Next up, we'll take a deeper look at the first of the big three wellness self-care factors: sleep. It's common wisdom that everyone needs their rest, but how does sleep figure in to all this brain chemistry via the workings of our Three Inner Bitches?

Sleep

Ah. Good ol' shut-eye. We all love it so much that we daydream about it. But do we ever truly prioritize getting it?

I know, I know. "This is boring, Shawna!" The kids, the job, the spouse, and the rare occasions you get to hang with the girlfriends—not to mention the overnight shifts!—all add up to less-than-optimal nighty-night time.

I get it—I worked nights and evenings most of my nursing career, but when I eventually switched to days, the entire landscape of my brain shifted. I literally felt like a fog had been cleared out of my head, and for the first time in a long time I was aware of what the heck was going on around me. My husband and kids initially did not appreciate this, as they had been running *Lord of the Flies* wild for years.

Turns out, my experience was rooted in—you guessed it—neuroscience. Our brains utilize a natural clearing system at night to rid themselves of the accumulated waste from daily thinking and plotting processes. Think of it like a computer hard drive set to automatically defrag itself (mind outta the gutter, ladies) every night. The glymphatic system efficiently washes away waste and toxic buildup, allowing us to process what happened during the day and to start the next one with a clean slate. Notably, when you do things that initiate new brain pathways (changing habits, moving forward through fear, etc.), the connections are built in the new action's moment, but the patterns are solidified during that night's wonderful sleep.

As you can imagine, this means that a good night's sleep plays a *crucial* role in the brain's ability to support long-term change in our lives. In fact, scientific studies have demonstrated that cognitive and motor skills can be negatively impacted by poor sleep.[1] Sleep deprivation has been shown to slow

---

1   Nir *et al.*, "Selective neuronal lapses precede human cognitive lapses following sleep deprivation," *Nature Medicine* 23, no. 12 (December 2017): 1474–1483, https://doi.org/10.1038/nm.4433.

down processing speeds, leading to lower-quality brain functioning, and it can significantly impair our ability to focus and pay attention.[2]

Changing your brain requires two important things related to the quality of your sleep. First, you need the ability to be a mindful observer of yourself in the moment, because often, the things we do that we wish we could change are things we do without paying much attention to them at all. For instance, maybe you frequently do things like agreeing to help a friend move because your habit is to say "yes," even when you have your own big plans. Or maybe you often find yourself eating chips while talking on the phone, without even noticing that you're doing it until you're halfway through the bag. When we are sleep-deprived, these actions seem to come even more out of the blue, sneaking up on us like ninjas trained in the ancient and deadly art of sabotage.

Secondly, long-term change requires commitment, even if it's just making small, incremental changes every day. This goes right out the window when we are exhausted and barely dragging our behinds through our habitual routines and day-to-day to-do lists, let alone when something novel is thrown into the mix. Sound judgment—a key factor in sticking to a commitment—is strongly affected by sleep deprivation, which is why we end up favoring Survival Bitch's impulsivity and cravings. This often leads us down the trail of choosing rewards that have us feeling better *now* versus those that align with Charge Bitch's well-considered long-term plans and goals.

And that's not all sleep deprivation does to our bodies and brains. It has also been repeatedly shown to negatively affect mood and has multiple

2   Paula Alhola and Päivi Polo-Kantola, "Sleep deprivation: Impact on cognitive performance," *Neuropsychiatric Disease and Treatment* 3 , no. 5 (October 2007): 553–567, https://www.ncbi.nlm.nih.gov/pmc/articles/PMC2656292/.

ties to impairing our psychological well-being. Additionally, when it comes to maintaining a healthy weight, chronic sleep deprivation will stack the deck against you. It increases your hunger hormone (ghrelin), decreases your satiety hormone (leptin), and prompts the brain-to-adrenal stress response, with its accompanying cortisol and belly fat production.[3] Yep, you're reading that right: not getting enough sleep literally contributes to that muffin top you've been trying to say goodbye to.

As with most things we do or do not do, sleep must be seen as a reward greater than the current one we are enjoying: Netflix, social media addiction, cocktails, you name it. Survival Bitch and Repetitive Bitch might be on any one of those party buses at midnight, living it up and loving it in the moment. But the next day, Charge Bitch will be spitting angry she couldn't come back with her usual witty repartee at the staff meeting, frustrated with the extra time it took to slog through payroll, and then too dead tired when she arrives home to even begin to plan anything that might resemble a meal for dinner. In other words, sleep deprivation derails goal setting and achievement and dramatically decreases your chances to make decisions that serve you best in the long term.

Long story short: If you want to start making lasting changes in your life, make time to get yourself into a good sleep routine. To this end, many of my clients develop a self-care checklist and incrementally add the things that work for them. Some popular techniques include taking three deep-breathing breaks during the day, meditating in the evening to settle down, and doing food prep for the rest of the week on the weekends so that they can take a little extra time to unwind after work on weeknights. If you just take twenty minutes in the eve-

---

3   Katherine Harmon, "How Slight Sleep Deprivation Could Add Extra Pounds," *Scientific American*, October 24, 2012, https://www.scientificameri-can.com/article/sleep-deprivation-obesity/.

ning to take a shower, put on some lotion, and stretch, the quality of your sleep should improve dramatically within a week or two. Many folks also find white noise helpful. Most importantly, do not take your phone to bed! That blue light is not good for your internal clock's sleeping rhythm.

Having a strong sleep routine in place is vital, but there's more than meets the eye to establishing a good self-care routine. You know that old maxim, "You are what you eat?" I think that one might have been coined after a Survival Bitch cookie binge turned Charge Bitch into Cookie Monster . . .

Diet

For many of us, the word "diet" alone summons forth a variety of emotions—from hope to dread to fear of yet another disappointment. Before you start to panic here, again, let's qualify our terms. When I talk about diet in this book, I'm not talking about keto, only eating orange food for a month, or measuring your self-worth based on a metal platform's digital display. I'm not talking about trying to lose weight on a white-knuckle, suck-the-joy-right-out-of-your-life deprivation diet.

Big nope!

While I'm no dietitian or nutritionist, I remain obsessively curious about any tool available to us that primes our body chemistry for positive change. Diet (as in, what we put into our bodies) has been shown repeatedly in the literature to be one of these factors. This is an obsession about *care*, not calories. Yes, it's about what you eat—but just as importantly, *how you view* what and why you eat matters.

Let me put it like this. As I've gotten older, I have begun to appreciate the great things my body and mind can still achieve. And on the days when things fall apart, it's often a result of less-than-optimal self-care in some form:

not taking breaks, neglecting to take time for fun, sleeping too little, avoiding meditation, or eating a diet lacking in the essential ingredients needed to function well and feel energized. Did you notice I didn't say "eating too much crap"? I said I wasn't eating enough food containing the vital essentials, and yes, reader, *that* is the key difference.

In essence, what we're talking about here is meeting your nutritional *and* psychological needs. The healthy and holistic way to go about this is with a slow but steady intentional addition of nutritious foods into your diet. I'll go into more detail about what to add and for what reason below, but let's stick with the big picture for the moment.

Once you've started to add in foods you know have good nutrition, notice how they affect your mood, energy, and general state of well-being. One thing you'll notice fairly quickly is that your attitude toward your diet starts to become focused on adding the good to crowd out the less good—rather than on depriving yourself of anything. If you keep this pattern up, there will be less room (and desire) for those foods that leave you feeling tired, cranky, or with an upset tummy—a state that doesn't foster the strength and energy for the change you really want.

In later chapters, we'll be discussing habits as they relate to working with the Three Inner Bitches, and if you want to use those tools for making changes to achieve permanent weight loss, you can. For now, in this section, you'll find a few diet-related topics that may shift your thinking on nutrition, how it impacts your daily function, and why you may want to reframe "diet" as giving yourself the nourishment you deserve.

Your Ticket to Nowhere on the Sugar Express

One of the most prevalent issues I see working against my clients' efforts in maintaining the stamina required to change up the routines and patterns that are no longer leading them in the direction they desire is the ol' sugar roller coaster. You know, eating bagels or pancakes at breakfast, pizza and subs for lunch, and pasta and breadsticks at dinner—and then a little dessert. This carb and sugar ride is less about excitement and more about frustration, irritability, and, ultimately, fatigue. You jump aboard when you regularly ingest simple, processed carbohydrates for food sources.

I know I sound judgy right now, but the reality is that this is the Standard American Diet (SAD). Now, I'm not trying to demonize any one food source, as that would go against everything I believe. But I do want to give you important information about this topic so *you* can decide what to do with it.

Imagine you started your morning with a quick, on-the-run meal, consisting mainly of processed carbs, sugar, and maybe caffeine. Your blood sugar spikes, and you get jolted with a nice glucose rush. You are singing aloud in traffic, pounding the steering wheel without a care in the world. "Come on, day! Let's go!" Your body's constant internal measurement devices sense this practically instantaneous bump in blood glucose levels. While dancing in your car may feel like a high energy-burning activity, unless you are running a marathon, all these carbs are likely to create a glucose response that is a tad too much for what your body requires in the moment. Your pancreas is sent in to respond to the higher blood glucose and save the day. It pumps out a jolt of insulin to move that excess sugar from the bloodstream and into your body's cells, where it is needed to keep your body's many processes functioning. Once your cells' demands are met, the excess sugar in your bloodstream is stored for later use in the liver, muscles, or fat cells. And guess what? If your existing fat cells are full, your body will create some new ones.

This relatively rapid lowering of blood glucose can make you feel like crap. This is commonly referred to as a sugar crash. "Never mind, day. You win." Common symptoms of this state range from dizziness to zapped energy and/or irritability to all-out hangry feelings.

Having fun yet? Not so much. This cycle can lead to not just weight gain, but hormonal issues, difficulty concentrating, anxiety, shakiness, binge eating, and one twisted, moody Survival Bitch. She is feeling jacked up and cranky and begins to ask herself, "What can make me feel better fast? Why, a cookie. Yes, a cookie can do the job." Buckle up, stay seated, and keep your arms and legs inside the vehicle. We are about to begin the round two ascent.

Now, note that this blood sugar roller coaster situation does not happen when we eat complex carbohydrates like oatmeal, beans, or barley, or foods with higher levels of proteins and healthy fats. These foods need digestive work to turn their particles into glucose energy, and the time passage works in your favor because you are likely fairly active, running the world and all. This slower digestion process prevents that rapid sugar spike and crash, as the energy is released into your bloodstream more slowly and used as you go about your day.

Unfortunately, many of us live on the sugar roller coaster all day every day, and it can lead to a continuous foggy, yucky feeling, blocking our ability to capture opportunities for change. By staying on this wild ride, we are setting ourselves up for disappointment, expecting to feel strong and powerful enough to choose new paths or accomplish difficult things when in fact we feel so freakin' tired and emotional—because we're not giving our bodies what they need so we can do the awesome new thing.

The Gut, the Bad, and the Ugly

Another useful nutrition concept to consider is that of your "second brain." It might surprise you to know I'm talking about your gut, which has its own nervous and communication system. It seems reasonable that there would be a communication system from your brain down to your gut, but I was really surprised when I learned there were actually nerve fibers traveling up *from* the gut, sending signals back up to the brain. Because of this two-way system, belly bloat' digestive issues and gut distress can literally lead to changes in your thinking and mental well-being.[4]

And our guts are not just used for digestion. The system that runs from our throats to our bums is made up of hundreds of millions of neurons and trillions of little bacteria, fungi, and viruses that live there. This is the little living factory called your microbiome. Our guts use the same neurotransmitters as our big ol' brains, sending messages via the vagus nerve back up to the brain, influencing how we feel in general. Yup: your belly can tell your brain what's up.

An estimated 95 percent of our serotonin and 50 percent of our dopamine is made in the gut. Serotonin helps regulate appetite and sleep, affects how you interpret pain, and plays a significant role in your emotional well-being. Dopamine is largely involved in pleasure, boosts mood, and plays a role in motivation, attention, learning, planning, and rewards. Other important brain chemicals and hormones are also found in your gastrointestinal tract. The production and release of these neurotransmitters and hormones is highly influenced by what type, variety, and ratio of good to bad germ species you have living in your gastrointestinal system. Your gut microbiome directly impacts not just your state of nourishment, but many other metabolic and disease factors. It can play a part in alleviating or worsening cortisol levels, inflammation, and your stress response. Multiple things can influence the makeup of your microbiome,

---

4   "The Brain-Gut Connection," John Hopkins Medicine, 2019, https://www.hopkinsmedicine.org/health/wellness-and-prevention/the-brain-gut-connection.

including the amount of daily stress you experience, the medicines you take, genetics, and your environment, but nutrition, if you are fortunate enough, is one you can control. And the good news? It is often hailed as one of the most influential, setting you up for all-over wellness and a seize-the-day attitude.

So how do you keep your gut happy?

First off, it's important to know that high-sugar, high-saturated-fat, processed foods can cause microbiome imbalance, which directly impacts mood in a negative way. On the other hand, regularly consuming a diverse range of plants in your diet produces the beneficial outcome of a more diverse microbiome.

There are also some specific things you can eat that are particularly helpful.

Probiotics are beneficial live bacteria already living inside your large intestines. They are useful in a range of ways, including helping to prevent harmful germs from invading, assisting with the further breakdown of food into usable forms, and aiding in the production of vitamins B_{12} and K. Scientific literature exists to support our ability to positively contribute to our probiotic environment by adding foods that naturally contain probiotics. These include fermented foods like kefir, pickled vegetables, tempeh, kombucha tea, sauerkraut, and high-quality yogurts.

Dietary fibers that are indigestible (by us, but not our microbiome) are often referred to as prebiotics. They help feed the probiotics in our gut. The more prebiotics that the probiotics have available to eat, the more efficiently they will work. Just a few examples of foods that contain these are onions, garlic, asparagus, bananas, and seaweed. Essentially, a diet full of fiber-rich foods like fruits or leafy greens, oats, and legumes will get you a good supply of prebiotics.

Polyphenols are antioxidants that act as fuel for the growth of these little wunderkind microbes. Some of the things you can consume that contain them include green tea, olive oil, apples, red wine, chocolate, and turmeric.

Brain Food

Adding more fuel to the "Gotta eat your real food!" fire is the fact that your brain needs lots of raw materials to make all the chemicals that allow you to think clearly and experience an upbeat, energetic mood. There are nine essential amino acids that play a big part here. These cannot be made by the body and therefore must come from food or supplements. Amino acids are often called the building blocks of proteins, but they are also vital in the synthesis of hormones and feel-good neurotransmitters like serotonin, dopamine, gamma-aminobutyric acid (GABA), and acetylcholine. If you are short on any of these building blocks (which are mainly derived from protein sources), it can negatively impact your mood, mental flexibility, attention, and memory. And if your thinking and concentration suffer, so do you, my friend. So do you.

B vitamins are essential to neurotransmitter creation. Vitamins B and C are required for feel-good brain chemical signals to be transmitted around your wonderful noggin. Many studies have also shown a link between vitamin D deficiency and mood, specifically anxiety and depression.

In Summary

Bottom line, I know it's no fun to hear it yet again, but a processed, low-nutritional-value diet can have negative effects, not just on maintaining a healthy weight but in many other important areas as well. For instance, Charge Bitch may experience cognitive deficits like faulty decision-making and an inability to think clearly. Even more painfully, when good nutrition gets derailed, Survival Bitch can get further knocked off her game due to a poor diet contributing to the already-hard symptoms of mood disorders such as depression and anxiety. There exists a whole field devoted to this subject called nutritional psychiatry.

These effects can impede or stop the progress you're making toward life changes. They can keep you from creating and adapting goals as you go and from maintaining a positive frame of mind while moving forward. They can also hamper your follow-through in times of challenge. Diet can set the stage well or poorly when it comes to molding your life to the one you really wish for. Change requires persistence and resilience. Optimizing your brain function with diet is hugely helpful to support your ideas, attitude, and performance in making great things happen.

At this point, I think you can see for yourself how food choices can help or halt your efforts in becoming a limitless, kick-ass Powerful Bitch. We're almost done in our world tour of Wellness Wonders. Next up, our last stop. Yep, we're gonna talk about moving your body.

Exercise

I am going to just go for it here and state boldly that regular exercise changes the structure and function of your brain in a positive direction. Brain change is often referred to as neuroplasticity. Neuroplasticity is the ability of areas of the brain to adapt, grow, and change based on what we expose them to and what we do with them habitually. When you intentionally choose actions that expose your brain to new ideas or routines for the purpose of creating new habits and pathways with something like consistent exercise, it is considered self-directed. I know this sounds like a tall order for your boring nine-year-old treadmill and that ThighMaster in the back of your closet. (Look it up, young ones! Worth it for the comedy gold of the infomercials alone.) But trust me, there's really something to this. And you don't have to take it just from me! Mental health experts often hail exercise as the number one thing a person can do to manage chronic stress, treat anxiety and depression, and prevent disease and cognitive decline. It also comes with a long list of other un-freakin'-believable brain benefits that will lead to you living a healthier, happier, and less stress-ridden life.

The first important way that exercise is known to improve brain functioning is to increase the production of chemicals known as "brain fertilizers." Yep, you read that right. I know it sounds wacky, but get a load of this: These fertilizers help stimulate brain activity in areas that have been shown to improve your brain's executive functioning (i.e., Charge Bitch's territory). As you might surmise, this is something you might find handy in your mom, wife, employee, all-hands-on-deck life. The most talked about of these brain fertilizers is brain-derived neurotrophic factor (BDNF). BDNF and other neurotrophic factors like it improve the function and promote the growth and survival of key brain cells and increase their stress resilience. Notably, stress can actually *decrease* the production of BDNF, so exercise is important to help counter stress's effects.

The second way that exercise is amazing for your brain is that it produces a mega dose of feel-good hormones and transmitters. The most well-known are endorphins, aka Mother Nature's morphine. The main function of endorphins is to inhibit the transmission of pain signals, but for most of us, they also produce a feeling of euphoria that improves our mood for the rest of the day. (Well, at least until the afternoon "brainstorming" meeting where your boss essentially vetoes everyone's suggestions except her own.) Endorphins, though, do not fully explain the so-called runner's high. There is compelling research that exercise can produce what is known as—and boy, this one is a mouthful—

endogenous cannabinoids.[5] These are the same chemicals in our body activated by cannabis or marijuana. Endocannabinoids alleviate pain, boost mood, reduce symptoms of worry and stress, and heighten sensations. (Sound familiar from your teenage experimentation days? Yeah, I see you.)

Exercise also triggers the release of dopamine, serotonin, and norepinephrine, which help with improving emotional regulation, brain functioning, and sleep. Low levels of dopamine, serotonin, and norepinephrine have been associated with depression, which is a big part of why exercise can help with this. It's worth noting that many antidepressant prescription drugs effectively work on the same principle, helping increase the availability of neurotransmitters in the brain. For example, Celexa, Lexapro, Prozac, Paxil, and Zoloft all do this. Wellbutrin is a norepinephrine-dopamine reuptake inhibitor (NDRI) and specifically boosts levels of the neurotransmitters norepinephrine and dopamine.

Not surprisingly, studies have shown lower rates of anxiety and depression among regular exercisers. Some studies have concluded that exercise works as well to alleviate mild to moderate depression as any other type of intervention. Regular exercise can also show you that you are capable of doing hard things and can help you to begin or end your day with a sense of accomplishment. Never forget that, even if you are not consciously aware of it, you are always at some level observing yourself. So, what you show that inner watcher can be seen as proof of what you're capable or not capable of achieving and matters much more than you may currently appreciate.

Boosting your mood isn't the only thing exercise does in conjunction

---

5   Siebers *et al.*, "Exercise-induced euphoria and anxiolysis do not depend on endogenous opioids in humans," *Psychoneuroendocrinology* 126 (April 2021): 105173, https://doi.org/10.1016/j.psyneuen.2021.105173.

with brain health. It's also an amazing way to improve both physical and mental resilience. Here's how: Exercise initially creates a stress response, producing hormones and chemicals like cortisol and epinephrine, which raise your heart rate and blood pressure, mimicking the physical process of stress, and when the exercise is over, mimicking the process of recovery from a stressful situation. Routine workouts offer us regular practice conditions for mental resilience because the physiological reaction in the body is the same one we go through during all kinds of stress responses. Once again, the body is matching the mind. In modern times, our brains have great difficulty parsing the difference between a bear chase and a nerve-racking employee performance review.

One of my favorite things that exercise improves is your brain's ability to pay attention. As you will see as we go further, attention is the money shot. Exercise and good cardiorespiratory fitness improve cognitive control and the ability to suppress distracting sensory information not related to the task at hand. This allows you to work past that text alert and make a mental note to check it later. Attention helps to prevent you from feeling the need to backtrack and double-check the work you just completed because you were scattered and only half present. Attention can stop you from rushing to "fix" everyone else's problems without even noticing until the deeds are done. Survival Bitch can also benefit from the good feels that can come when she can truly capture moments of authentic joy and human connection.

Attention is where the power lies to create the *pause to choose* the best path.

So many times, the behaviors and routines we wish we could adopt or quit happen or do not happen when we are living most of our days on autopilot.

In conclusion, exercise helps boost executive function and improves processing speeds, inhibitory control, learning, memory, problem-solving, decision-making, and perception. It has positively been shown to increase information processing speed for a period of up to two hours afterward. All of this is extremely helpful when it comes to Charge Bitch's goal setting and achievement. Bottom line, routine exercise really helps to set the stage for the energy needed to sustain the motivation and grit to achieve the things that matter, and, with consistency, Repetitive Bitch wouldn't have it any other way.

America Runs on Self-Care

When it comes down to it, any time we humans ignore our ancestral, biological, or circadian rhythms or our nutritional and movement needs built on ages of genetic coding, we are bound to create physiological and mental stress. No matter how evolved we like to believe we have become, this is no less true now than it was a long time ago for our ancestors.

As you set out on your journey to become the Powerful Bitch of your dreams, food, exercise, and sleep routines become small but vital pieces in the larger scheme of maintaining the beautiful machine that is your body and mind. In my experience, respect and kindness to both are necessary. After all, both are often needed to create the moments that offer peak satisfaction, presence, and happiness. Both offer the instruments to create your own form of success. Remember, suboptimal foundations can't hold up big dreams.

And please, never underestimate the power of how we all tend to view our own habits of self-care. Even without consciously noting it, we still perceive our everyday seemingly small actions or inactions as helping or hurting our often already existing mind/body suffering. Treating ourselves with kindness will impact our beliefs surrounding self-worth because our minds thirst for congruency in all aspects of self-care. After all, if you figuratively eat crap and accept less-than-respectful treatment from others, it can become difficult to fully buy into nourishing and caring for your body, as at some level you are absorbing the message that you are not worth it.

You *are* worth it. After all, you're a Powerful Bitch—or on your way to becoming one.

In the next chapter, we'll explore how stress tanks our efforts to create positive change by dampening Charge Bitch's presence. We'll also explore some popular ways women try to deal with stress that unfortunately *do not work*, and how to implement best-practice stress-management techniques instead.

CHAPTER THREE:

MANAGING STRESS, OR HOW TO AVOID "CHARGE BITCH HAS LEFT THE BUILDING!"

"Just when you feel you have no time to relax, know that
this is the moment you most need to make time to relax."
— Matt Haig, *Reasons to Stay Alive*

Grab the Tiger by the Teeth

Imagine, if you will, the distant origins of Survival Bitch: your cavewoman self. Can you see her yet? She is rocking a killer saber-toothed-tiger-fur dress and has a baby slung over one shoulder in what looks like a woolly-mammoth-fur backpack. Cavewoman Survival Bitch survived hostile environments with vigilance and feminine warrior strength. She watched for sudden movements while walking down grassy paths, searching for nuts and berries. She listened for new noises while hunting to feed her family. And she was *amazing* at keeping your cavewoman self safe from the dangers of Stone Age life. After all, that's the stuff Survival Bitch was designed to do.

You know what Cavewoman Survival Bitch didn't have to deal with, though? And what she wasn't designed to guard against? Running the gauntlet that the twenty-first century has you dealing with every day. You know, your busy, hectic schedule that starts with making lunches while doing your hair in the kitchen, driving the kids to school while talking to a colleague on the phone and fighting traffic to get to work on time. And all this before nine a.m.!

Hectic, busy situations would have been highly unusual for Cavewoman Survival Bitch. Today we have calls, texts, traffic, and noise pollution. We also have financial and societal demands to do it all, and do it well, or risk losing our jobs, our houses, our marriages, and our standing in the community. And we'd better be prepared to juggle this twenty-four hours a day. (Oof, my heart rate is going up even just writing this.)

Now, the stress response hardwired to Survival Bitch's command center is efficient for getting us through temporary situations, like running from a burning building, but it is not where you need to be in dealing with everyday things like work, kid issues, and your mother-in-law. Your cavewoman self was not running *all damn day* from that saber-toothed tiger.

But here's the kicker: When you're in a state of chronic stress, your body and your brain chemistry respond like that tiger is actually there, right behind you and ready to pounce. And it's nigh impossible to make good decisions and execute on Charge Bitch's awesome plans toward Powerful Bitchhood with a thousand pounds of fur, claws, and teeth breathing down your neck.

Understanding how stress affects us is half the battle in learning to manage it. As for the rest? You guessed it: keep reading.

Charge Bitch Has Left the Building

It might not surprise you to learn that inability to manage stress is the number one reason clients come to me for help.

Now, my three favorite definitions of stress are as follows:

- A demand for change.
- An overestimation of danger and an underestimation of our ability to cope with it.
- The load is too great to bear, or our *perception* is that the load is too great to bear.

Not being able to get a handle on this stuff is the wholly understandable reason why many women cannot access Charge Bitch in crucial moments and use her rational intelligence to play a vital role in becoming a Powerful Bitch.

What I've learned is that one of the biggest factors in creating and perpetuating stress is the subconscious stories playing out inside our heads about our stress . . . and our shortcomings in dealing with it. These powerful messages are cycled over and over again, like having similarly themed fear-based news stories broadcasting within your mind throughout the day—only instead of world news, it's all predictions about how things might go wrong for you in the near or distant future. We often do this with the best of intentions. "I'm just trying to mentally prepare myself for what I might have to deal with later," we think. But the reality is that allowing ourselves to focus on the negative things that *may* or *may not* happen causes a never-ending cycle of stress. Our brains and bodies get the constant message that danger is coming, or that it is already here, receiving messages to expect and prepare for the almost inevitability of our physical or psychological needs not getting met. The result of this is a state of chronic stress—and that's where things really start to get hairy. Like, the aforementioned thousand pounds of fur, claws, and teeth hairy.

Chronic stress is our body's natural response to danger gone into over-drive. For far too many of us, though, being stressed out has become an ongoing, miserable, and yet expected way of life.

Of course, the stories playing out in our heads aren't our only source of stress. Events like the loss of a job or family member, fractured significant relationships, and massive life change, by nature, cause stress. Something I hear myself saying to clients is, "You can't completely reverse a normal response." If you're ridiculously overscheduled and not supported or validated, then no tips, tools, or strategies are going to be enough to fully repair that. That often requires a significant change in support systems and circumstances for truly effective relief.

Even so, while you're in that crisis mode, you can still learn to tamp down the sense of overwhelm enough to gain the strength to weather the storm and the Charge Bitch clarity needed to carry out a few actionable and manageable steps, as appropriate. With this effort, Survival Bitch will gain confidence in her own self-regulation and coping tools, which—let me tell you—is immeasurably valuable.

In this chapter, I hope to help you to gain some insight on the likely sources and root causes of your biggest stressors. You'll also walk away with a better understanding of how to notice stress when it first shows up and how to diminish its impact on the quality of your life using a variety of tools that are already available to you—you might just not have realized it. Once you start using these tools to curb the stress response while you're in it, you'll feel more confidently able to tackle the lasting changes you want to make in your life on your quest to become a Powerful Bitch.

Stress Response: What Is It? And How to Identify It

The ability to identify when your body goes into a stress response is critical to maintaining your ability to keep Charge Bitch (i.e., the most wise and logical part of yourself) in the building. Any time you catch your worried thoughts propagating before your body becomes overly amped up, or vice versa, you can respond wisely versus reacting . . . well, you know. When you can switch your focus and attention to something in the present moment like the breath, or a comfortable area in the body, it will lessen the intensity of the worry loops in your brain and prevent the hijack of your nervous system function.[6] (More on these and other specific tools and tricks to short-circuit the stress response coming later in this chapter!)

So, what exactly is the "stress response"? In a nutshell, it's your sympathetic nervous response, which is governed by a branch of your autonomic nervous system. This is the system responsible for the fight, flight, or freeze response. You know, Survival Bitch's domain.

The stress response can be triggered in a variety of ways. It can happen when Survival Bitch's Spidey-Sense picks up any hint of danger, kicking her fear center into gear and priming you to be ready to fight, flee, or freeze to keep you alive. Unfortunately, it can also happen when Charge Bitch's self-referencing center conjures up imagined thoughts of impending danger that, for all intents and purposes, seem just as real and urgent—even when they're just thoughts and fears given voice inside your head, instead of actual tigers. In both cases, signals are sent lightning-fast to another brain area under Survival Bitch's domain, as well as to key organs in your body. Before you know it, you've got yourself a full-body chemical shitstorm: a sympathetic nervous system hijack.

When this happens, signals are sent from the brain to the adrenal glands, ordering them to pump out the hormone epinephrine (better known as adrenaline) into the bloodstream on the double. This is one powerful drug. It will jack

6   "Focus More to Ease Stress," Harvard Health, 2011, https://www.health.harvard.edu/healthbeat/focus-more-to-ease-stress.

up your heart rate, blood pressure, and breathing. Increased amounts of oxygen start flowing to your brain, vital organs, and large muscles. You are now on high alert. Epinephrine also gets your energy stores and liver pumping out glucose into your bloodstream. Digestion slows because you need to save that energy for the fight-to-the-death battle your body is priming itself for. It may be the case that you are actually about to start running away from a mugger—but what you are facing may also be something you interpret in the moment as equally life-threatening, for instance, doing your first live video on social media for your business.

The stress response has other effects on the mind and body too. Sexual desire diminishes. ("Sorry, honey, I'm having a heart attack.") Your senses are sharpened, and you may jump easily at sudden movements or sounds. The TV suddenly seems *really* loud.

As I mentioned before, knowing what to look for to identify a stress response is half the battle. Once you notice signs like rapid, shallow breathing, irritability, shoulder tension, or maybe a racing heart, you know that you're in a stress response. This can happen so fast you don't even consciously realize it. In other instances, my clients experience something we call "stress creep." This occurs with the layering of micro-stress moments as they accumulate during the day, starting with something like awakening to the feel of cat puke squishing between your toes as your feet hit the floor first thing in the morning. Unfortunately, the result is complete overload by nightfall, taking a good night's sleep off the table and, you know . . . adding more fuel to the stress fire. Being able to see the stress response when it first begins to gather momentum gives you the opportunity to do something about it before it gets any worse.

And unfortunately, it *can* get worse, physiologically speaking.

The Effects of Long-Term Stress

What we've been talking about so far are the effects of immediate, short-term stress. But a funny thing happens when we experience an extended stress response, like chronic stress. Chronic stress is commonly caused by ongoing issues like financial problems within a marriage or working in a career you entered to meet other people's expectations, as opposed to doing with your life whatever would really make *you* happy. Signs of chronic stress include an inability to relax or enjoy things like you used to, an overwhelming sense of fatigue, chronic GI issues, and loss of the ability to muster a healthy perspective (i.e., little issues start to seem much bigger and scarier than they really are).

That last one, perspective loss, is a doozy. When you're under stress, your focus actually narrows, creating sort of a tunnel vision effect where you can't help but be laser-focused on noticing all the potential negative outcomes versus positive possibilities. Some scientists think your vision literally changes. If you look at the horizon outside, it can actually help with this. It encourages that much-needed peripheral vision. After all, many answers in life are not found directly in front of you.

What's happening here in Inner Bitch terms is that stress kicks Repetitive Bitch and Survival Bitch into gear. And these two are not cheering for betterment or change. They are voting for keeping the status quo because that's a low-energy strategy that has been shown to keep you alive in the past—and because you're stressed out, they assume you need to preserve all the energy you can right now to deal with whatever monstrous thing is stressing you out.

If whatever is causing your stress response continues, other areas of the brain start sending messages to your adrenals to produce more of the infamous stress chemical cortisol. Cortisol prompts further elevations in blood glucose to give you the ongoing energy you apparently need to save yourself from the saber-toothed tiger . . . all day, every day. Doesn't sound great, right?

Unfortunately, long-term stress response contributes to metabolic syndrome, which leads to an increased amount of visceral belly fat and issues with blood pressure and cholesterol. If not turned around, it can evolve into even worse issues, like diabetes, heart disease, and polycystic ovarian syndrome.[7]

When we experience chronic stress, Survival Bitch's fear center becomes more active, to the point that this heightened stress state can become your new normal. You feel jittery and more easily overwhelmed. You can also add to the layers of your negativity bias because "Hey, we are in a crisis! So that is what we should be scanning the environment for, right?" Your mind begins to assume that you are always in danger, noticing the negative quickly, proving yourself right that bad stuff could happen, altering your thoughts and mood. You may begin to discount and filter out wonderful options before you even realize they are there. You may feel a persistent desire to flee or escape. If this goes on for any length of time, it is common to feel irritable, be less empathetic, and have difficulties in social settings. Concentration and focus suffer. Worst of all, reaching this state turns the stress response into something of a vicious cycle: the fight, flight, or freeze response seems to get locked in.

At this point, Survival Bitch becomes by far the loudest and most dominant member of the team, allowing Repetitive Bitch on the field only to pull out old, tired playbook moves . . . unless you master the tools you need to calm her. We'll get to those later in this chapter, but first up, let's look at how stress affects Charge Bitch's superpowers.

---

7   Karen Ryan, "Stress and Metabolic Disease," in *Sociality, Hierarchy, Health: Comparative Biodemography: A Collection of Papers,* ed. M Weinstein, MA Lane (Washington, DC: National Academies Press, 2014).

Stress: Charge Bitch's Kryptonite

Charge Bitch, as you already know, has shortcomings when it comes to her performance. She is not perfect, and we would all breathe a little easier in life if we curtailed that expectation. Charge Bitch is logical, yes, but what makes her human is her power of imagination. This is also what makes her occasionally superhuman in her ability to envision a better future for us and then make a plan to go and actually get that future.

However, this power of imagination can be used for the forces of evil as well as for good—which is to say, Charge Bitch's gifted imagination can take us in directions that are not always the most helpful. She also may be working with a few baked-in (mis)perceptions about her capacities and shortcomings. The combination of these things can lead her into that worrying routine I mentioned previously—you know, the worst fortune-teller version of the nightly news, constantly on a reel inside your head? Yeah. That's Charge Bitch losing her shit.

Now, Charge Bitch doesn't mean to stir the worry pot. She's just trying to avoid painful fallout by analyzing potential self-related problems, because that is, after all, how she's wired. The strategic planner. The origins of this worry routine may be Charge Bitch starting a thought process with something benign and simple like: "Oh yeah, I have to present at the roundtable this week. Do you suppose they expect slides? What should I wear? I hope my face doesn't get fire-engine red. Shit." Underneath this is a fear of being judged harshly or rejected. Next up: "How can I *avoid* this so Survival Bitch doesn't get hurt? Should I call in sick?" Other times, it might go a little like: "What did I do in this situation? Why did I do that? How did I make it worse?" or, "What will people think about me when I quit my respectable job? How will I screw up my kid? Why did I say that at the women's group? Do you suppose they are still talking about it?"

Does any of this sound familiar? I'm willing to bet it does. And if that's the case, you know exactly the kind of negative thought spiral I'm talking about.

The problem with the mental exercise of thinking through how everything might go wrong is that it activates Survival Bitch via tension, heart palpitations, and other not-so-fun symptoms, further cementing the idea that something bad is *definitely* going down. Not later, but *right now*.

This tricky little area is what mental health and neuroscience experts like to call the "self-reference center" or "self-focused negative thinking." That is a fancy way of saying that Charge Bitch's mind takes things a little too far, wandering off to the valley of death. Here, Charge Bitch unintentionally uses her power of imagination against herself. Next, Survival Bitch receives these unsettling messages and—understandably—reacts exactly as she is programmed to react.

Another way people experience this is using Charge Bitch's powers of imagination to guess (or perhaps catastrophize) what the future holds, then scramble trying to anticipate all the problems of tomorrow, next week, or even, say, your kid's wedding (even though your kid is only five). This is a multistep, six-degrees-of-Kevin-Bacon brand of worrying, and many of my clients find themselves doing this all day every day.

A quick way to help you identify the difference between runaway-train-Charge Bitch-type worry and engaging in productive planning is to pause and check your body, just like we talked about before. Look for a churning sensation or an ache in your gut, the tightness between your shoulder blades, or the rapidity of your heartbeat. If any of that stuff is happening, there's a good chance what you're actually doing is worrying, not planning. Worrying about judgment from others if you mess up or misstep feels very different than mapping out a strategy with facts. Planning is something Charge Bitch does logically, with a calm, clear intent, a steady heartbeat, and a cup of tea. Check your body and know your mind.

And of course, all this future-tripping can be done so often it becomes Repetitive Bitch's territory. Immerse yourself in daily chronic worry from one minute to the next and, before you know it, that will be how you spend most of your days, one simple negative thought acting as the cue to unravel many more.

When stress comes in and stays in, sadly, the mission becomes small and immediate. No big dreams. No grand plans. The gate to endless possibilities closes and we find ourselves just going with the first thing that saves us the energy needed for decision-making. In comes Repetitive Bitch, enticing you with all her sexy, low-energy habits, thought patterns, and well-worn neural grooves. You can follow her steps with your eyes closed, and they are perfectly suited for chaotic times—even though they ultimately all lead down the same path to the very large rut you've been feeling stuck in.

The good news is that it doesn't have to be like this—or, if it is like this now, it doesn't have to *stay* like this. Next up, we're going to talk about some of the ways we tend to try to deal with stress that just plain don't work.

How Not to Deal with Stress

One big area where folks tend to go wrong in trying to manage stress is that they focus solely on the external events in their lives that are contributing to stress, rather than considering their own self-efficacy when it comes to dealing with stressors. The reality is that life is stressful sometimes—that doesn't change. What we can change, though, is how we cope with it when it happens.

We'll talk more about effective coping techniques later in this chapter. For now, let's discuss some of the most common methods my clients use to try to manage stress that they ultimately find to be unhelpful in the long term.

Distraction

I often see clients attempt to use distraction to dim or block the negative feelings of stress, rather than using tools that reset the body to a "rest and digest" space. I recognize this in them because I know the pattern from my own history. It is akin to using Tylenol for a UTI. In other words, it may cover up the symptoms *temporarily*, but it doesn't solve the core issue, and in both cases the pain will return.

Sometimes it is hard for people to differentiate between "working" and distractions. Working is obviously a productive activity and, yes, can serve as a distraction, preventing runaway worry loops, but Charge Bitch can't perform at a high executive level in perpetuity and will eventually need a "break." And giving yourself a time-out from thinking work and allowing this mind-wandering, self-referential time is not always a bad thing. It is a wonderful source of purpose- and meaning-making, which are so valuable in life.

Additionally, distractions do have their place in the short term—for instance, in overwhelming public situations. After all, if you started chanting mantras and got into the lotus position during the middle of a staff meeting, it might raise a few eyebrows. But in the long term, consistently and solely relying on distractions will not only prevent you from returning to a calm state but will lead you to the point of needing more and more distraction in order to feel okay, as quiet begins to feel uncomfortable—or, in the worst cases, intolerable.

So, what are some popular choices for distraction or numbing? Some of the most common ones I see are wine, gossiping, busyness, social media, gambling, overworking, and overeating sweet foods. Me? I had a good run with busyness. Like . . . a good twenty-plus-years run. I felt like I was treading water in a huge ocean and was so, so tired. All the time. But I didn't know how to stop for fear that I would just go under. I never knew I could surf the waves.

This is not to say I am now perfect and always in tune with the rumblings of my soul. I can still play the distraction game like a three-card monte champion, but I do less of it. I am getting better at processing my days' positive and negative experiences honestly, instead of always trying to avoid them. In the past, the discomfort patiently remained anyway, until I actually paused for a moment and it popped back up into awareness. I lost a lot of the gifts of the present moment during that time of distraction, moments I can never get back. I lost moments like on Christmas morning, when I was worrying about keeping on top of the trash pile of wrapping paper and ribbon instead of plunking my bottom on the couch and soaking up my kids' joy. I lost moments by doing dishes and cleaning floors when my boys were little and just wanted to go to the park, or by half-listening to school-day stories while I worried about what my nursing night shift assignment might look like.

When I found awareness and learned how to really get into the beauty of these moments, it took me aback, and I had to take time to forgive myself for missing them in the first place.

Multitasking

This is the other big tactic I see my clients trying to use to manage stress. And while it may seem like it is helping, for the most part, it does not. The way I view it, the only time multitasking works is if you're using two different Bitches at once. For example, you can fold laundry with Repetitive Bitch while Charge Bitch plans dinner. You can knit, sew buttons, or iron clothes (Repetitive Bitch territory if you already know how) and also watch the weather with Charge Bitch and plan what clothes to pack for your girls' weekend. You can staple pamphlets (Repetitive Bitch has this on lock!) while strategizing your marketing plan (guess who?).

But what about reading a text while talking to someone? Or constantly checking emails on your phone while others are chatting in the near vicinity? Let's face it: In either scenario, someone is going to get only half of your attention, and you will end up feeling a little scattered and pressured, even if only for a few seconds. That's because, if you ask Charge Bitch to concentrate on two things at the same time, it just doesn't work well. As a result, asking this of Charge Bitch bumps up your stress a little notch at a time. And we do that all day. We even *pride* ourselves on our ability to multitask, when most of the things we try to actually do while multitasking don't get done to the best of our ability and leave us feeling even more ragged around the edges, rather than less so.

Remember that your cavewoman self was not trying to decide, plan, judge, and analyze two things at once. She might have been shucking berries while grunting at the cave kids or mentally designing masterpieces on cave walls while doing primitive laundry, but she was not using her Charge Bitch for multiple thinking tasks simultaneously.

It may not seem like it, but ultimately you save time (and your peace of mind) if you focus solely on the task at hand—even rapidly *moving* from one to the next. So please don't try to do your taxes while taking work calls. Something is bound to go wrong.

In chapter 4, we're going to talk about beginning a mindfulness practice, which will give you a greater ability to focus on each task as it comes, finish it, and quickly move to the next without doubting, checking, and worrying if you completed it fully and correctly. (Perfectionists out there, again I'm looking at you!)

Now that we've looked at some common ways that we try and fail to deal with stress, let's move on to some methods that actually work! But first, we'll take a quick look at the physiological markers of a state of calm and learn how keeping your chill benefits your health and overall wellness.

From Fight-Flight-Freeze to Rest and Digest

For the moment, let's concentrate on physiological calm—the state that should resume naturally when the immediate threat and danger have passed and your mind and body have processed the "all clear" signal. Your brain should return to being under the influence of more calming neurotransmitters, like serotonin and GABA. Your breathing slows, your heart rate and blood pressure decline, and your libido and digestion can resume proper functioning.

You can think of this mode as "rest and digest," which exists at the complete opposite end of the spectrum from "fight, flight, or freeze." The rest and digest response maintains calm and wellness, allowing for a blood pressure reading that helps keep your physician's script pad firmly in their pocket. The more time you spend in this state, the more you reap a host of health and wellness benefits. Truly, you can prevent an astounding number of modern-day ills and issues that so many people struggle with due to chronic inflammation brought on by an unrelenting stress cycle.

During rest and digest, Charge Bitch returns to the scene to offer her wisdom, and Survival Bitch feels safe and settled. You become more open to opportunities, positivity, empathy, and creativity. It is hard to imagine, but we are supposed to be in this parasympathetic state most of the time. Our bodies and minds are designed to do our highest work while in it.

So it's not hard to begin to understand why a state of chronic stress really throws us for a loop on every level—physically, mentally, and emotionally. Now, as promised, let's look at some short-term tools you can use to counteract your fight-flight-freeze response and find your way quickly back to rest and digest.

A Better Way to Deal with Stress

As I mentioned, the entire next chapter is devoted to mindfulness, an ultimate long-term stress-reliever. Even so, I did promise I'd arm you with a toolkit of things you can use to calm your own stress response on a daily basis—some even while it's actually happening. These short-term tools are great because they are portable and available on demand, which allows you to turn the stress train around before it has gone too far down the track. Once your stress response is in full gear, it is much harder to navigate back to baseline, and you might actually forget there are things you can do to reset yourself. This puts you in a place to make better decisions in the moment. These tools are also useful because they help us to regularly practice self-soothing to counterbalance the daily rigors of life that most of us endure. It may not seem like it, but our daily interactions, environment, background noise level, and the sheer volume of decisional points we manage every day pile up and cause stress that oftentimes goes unnoticed . . . until problems like insomnia, digestive ailments, or chronic fatigue hit us like a ton of bricks.

If you can start to adopt some of these strategies now and see what works best for you, you'll be developing tools to have in your arsenal to garner that crucial sense of confidence to know that you *do* possess the skills of self-management needed for peace.

Here are a few simple ways to *intentionally* engage the parasympathetic nervous system on a regular basis:

- Spending time with and petting animals
- Praying
- Immersing yourself in positive, pleasurable sensory experiences, like a warm bubble bath or listening to music you love
- Exercising

- Playing with children
- Laughing authentically
- Engaging in meditative or mindfulness practices
- Doing yoga
- Spending time in nature, creating a sense of awe
- Cultivating rapport. This can be as simple as a really good conversation where you truly feel connected to another human being.
- Practicing gratitude by keeping a gratitude journal or list

All of the above are useful tools to have at your disposal, and some you can use in the moment to counteract a stress response. I like to tell my clients that there are behavioral levers under their control that they can push and pull to change their state, and they find this very empowering. Taking a moment to pet your dog, share a funny story from your day with a friend, or play with your child can do wonders for your mental and physiological state. Below, I'm going to expand on a few especially helpful tools I'd like you to have in your kit to manage stress on a day-to-day basis.

Gratitude

Gratitude practices are a wonderful way to counteract stress and its pull to focus on the negative. The human brain has to filter incoming environmental information because we can't possibly process and pay full attention to all the things we see, hear, smell, taste, and touch throughout our days. If we tried, we would suffer from a sensory processing overload. Negativity bias is normal. Gratitude helps nudge us gently to correct that bias and foster positivity and happiness. You will gain more benefit from gratitude journaling if you don't write down items as they occur but make your list at a specific time of day, every day. Getting into this routine forces your brain to really notice and savor experiences as they occur, squirreling them away in your mind for later recall in writing.

Additionally, without specific guidance, the brain will *perceive* your current situation and state based on what you're wired to expect, seek, and notice day in and day out, based on your experiences from the past. Your current mood can also change this perception. As we discussed earlier, if you feel stressed, you'll notice more dangerous situations, annoying people, or events. If you're lighthearted, the opposite is true. Again, negativity bias (the tendency for our brains to quickly notice and highlight negative events more than the positive) playing a role. It's hardwired into us because danger will kill, and our continuation as a species relies on us giving it the highest priority. (Survival Bitch to the rescue! Sort of . . .)

Gratitude listing has scientific support in its ability to improve negative mood states.[8] Gratitude has also been shown to improve emotional intelligence and produce a host of positive brain chemicals that buffer stress.[9] If I told you I had a pill that would produce those same effects, and described what it would do, I bet you would pay a lot of money to get your hands on it. People worry that if they become grateful for what they have, they may lose their drive to pursue goals and become complacent, but the opposite is true. Because gratitude buffers stress, it allows you to gear up again and replenish your motivation. And, best yet, this practice is free and takes just a few moments of your time each day.

---

8   Ducasse *et al.*, "Gratitude diary for the management of suicidal inpatients: a randomized controlled trial," *Depression and Anxiety* 36, no. 5 (May 2019): 400–411, https://doi.org/10.1002/da.22877.

9   Madhuleena Roy Chowdhury, "The Neuroscience of Gratitude and How It Affects Anxiety & Grief," PositivePsychology.com, October 9, 2021, https://positivepsychology.com/neuroscience-of-gratitude/.

Offering Acts of Kindness

This topic could be a book on its own. Many of us go through our days performing what, for all appearances, seem to be acts of kindness or service, unfortunately at times to the extreme or for the wrong reasons and therefore to our detriment. The benefits of offering acts of kindness are extraordinary, but only if the motivation is authentically altruistic. The litmus test is within you, and we will dig deeper into that sticky wicket as we go further. In the meantime, the question you can begin to ask yourself is: "Why do I routinely do or say 'nice' things?"

Well, before you say, "Duh, Shawna. Because I *am* nice," please consider something. Are you acting out of a genuine desire to connect with someone else in a spirit of giving, or is it out of a fear of not being liked or needed? Or is it possible you're helping or giving out of the fear of being judged as selfish if you don't? Trust me, you will experience an entirely different chemical response and sense of satisfaction from the exact same set of actions when they're done for different reasons. When you act out of altruism, Survival Bitch feels warm, cuddly, and connected to community. Alternatively, when you do for others out of a sense of fear of judgment or rejection, you may find yourself feeling resentful, annoyed, angry, frustrated, and eventually just plain tired. Please don't calculate your worthiness based on what you *do* for others over who you *are*.

Breath Work

Deep breathing works at so many levels to reset your system to a relaxed state. It is my favorite tactic, by far, in stress-management techniques, since I appreciate any tool that offers freedom. For those of us blessed to be healthy, the breath is always available and does not rely on anything or anyone else. The quality and cadence of the breath is often a mirror of how we are experiencing and perceiving our environment and the inner dialogue we are creating around it. If you pay close attention to the breath and the general sensations within your chest area, it can offer insight on specific scenarios and individuals that inspire a sense of calm or joy. It can also clue you in to those that bring about the opposite, causing tightness in the chest, tension in the jaw, or a general sense of unease or dread.

There is, of course, physiology involved in taking slow diaphragmatic (i.e., deep) belly breaths. The human heart contains chemical receptors that measure the amount of oxygen in the blood being pumped throughout your body. If oxygen is noted to be low, as in the case of rapid shallow breathing (or in the case of anemia or dehydration or other health issues), your heart rate is elevated to compensate for the lack of available oxygen and nutrients needed to maintain cell life at every level.

Breath work helps to correct this. Additionally, it activates the vagus nerve, which goes through the diaphragm. The vagus nerve stimulates the release of an amazing calming chemical called acetylcholine, sending signals to the brain that all is well and promoting relaxation. I view the practice of deep breathing as a portable, on demand, calming rescue drug. It calls Charge Bitch back into the game, helping you make the best decisions available in the moment of a stressful event, versus later when you wish you had acted differently.

Take five intentional slow belly breaths now and see if there is a difference in how you feel. Or do "box" breathing: breathe in while counting to four, slowly. Hold that breath for another count of four. Then breathe out slowly for another count of four and hold again for four.

My new favorite game-changing breath technique is called the physiological sigh. To perform this one, fill the lungs using two separate nasal inhales (halfway with the first and all the way with the second), then exhale longer through the mouth. My clients and I like to make an audible sigh (or groan) sound when exhaling.

These and many other techniques are available on YouTube if you prefer a visual demonstration.

It is crucial (like, remembering-to-use-your-30-percent-off-coupon-before-it-expires crucial) to practice your breathing techniques during everyday moments and not wait until you're already feeling completely overwhelmed. Once a big "freak the freak out" situation goes down, it will not occur to you to take a deep breath if you haven't already been practicing. But if you perform deep breathing regularly and repeatedly with a resulting calm response, Survival Bitch feels better and becomes assured that this tool is a reliable source for self-soothing. At that point, Repetitive Bitch will say, "How about we habit this? It seems to be preventing some serious shit shows."

Bringing It All Together

To sum up what we've learned in this chapter:

- You can't both experience nonstop pings and dings from all of your devices *and* relax.

- You can't attempt to focus on fifteen things per second and perform and concentrate well or do so without ending up feeling scattered and stressed out.

- You have within you the power to identify when you start to experience a stress response and nip that sucker in the bud with tools like deep breathing and taking a moment for yourself before your biochemistry gets out of hand and sends Charge Bitch running from the building while Survival Bitch's responses signal Repetitive Bitch to break out the ice cream and the *One Tree Hill* reruns.

Skeptical?

If you are thinking, "This is ridiculous and this woman does not understand just how stressful my life is right now," I hear ya, and I feel ya. My past skepticism was as large as our wine store tab during the shelter-in-place part of COVID-19. But the science behind the stress response versus the relaxation response swayed me. If you can change your physiological response, you change your body chemistry, your thinking, and therefore your life. As I like to tell my clients, "If you can practice the art of living in calm, it is a much further road back to freak-out mode, buying you time to change course."

The ability to command "rest and digest" allows Charge Bitch to contribute great ideas and expansive possibilities. Getting out of the chronic stress state is fundamental in creating the space to even begin to make neurological change, which *is* permanent self-change. Sadly, it is almost impossible to consider significant self-betterment when living moment by moment in survival mode.

We are aiming to get you in the space to really begin to be radically curious about your mindsets, to begin to challenge false beliefs and assumptions, and, most of all, to begin to do the brave things needed to create your best and most Powerful Bitch self.

The best version of ourselves is often drowned out amid chaos and stress.

Give her a moment of stillness, a deep breath, and she will come forth.

She was there all along.

In the next chapter, we'll deep dive into the long-term stress management—along with many other life-changing benefits that comes from adopting a regular mindfulness practice. After all, a Powerful Bitch is, above all else, a Mindful Bitch.

CHAPTER FOUR

MINDFULNESS: THE BIRD'S-EYE VIEW OF INNER BITCH ACTIONS

"We have become so highly conditioned by our patterns of thinking
that we don't even recognize thoughts as thoughts anymore."
— Jon Kabat-Zinn, *Mindfulness for Beginners*

A Precious Moment Lost

It was the day of my son's high school graduation ceremony. I was in the stands with my husband, my parents, our other three sons, and our two daughters-in-law. As I sat there, I was suddenly aware of a heavy numbness in my chest. Not so much a feeling, but more of a *lack* of feeling—an absence of joy that contrasted with what I was seeing from the other people around me. They were smiling, laughing, thoroughly enjoying the moment. As I realized this, I was struck with a feeling of separateness. I wanted so very much to be fully there and in the moment with everyone else, but I just wasn't.

In my mind, I tried to replay cherished memories of our boy from birth up to that day, but they just couldn't fully take hold in my heart space. Instead, my mind kept zooming back in on preparations I had made or still needed to make for the party we'd be hosting at our house in just a few hours—all the balloons, food, and other essentials. Did I have enough? Was the house clean enough? Would people have fun?

I was so wrapped up in thinking through those minor worries that I couldn't fully appreciate or really *be in* this awesomely momentous experience. And here's the kicker: this was worsened by the fact that I was consciously aware of what I was failing to do—to be present in a very precious moment. By this point, I had already been practicing living presently for a few years, and I knew all too well what I was missing. More importantly, I knew I was robbing my boy of what he really wanted and deserved: a mom who was engaged, her heart full and her eyes lit up with love and pride.

So how had I found myself in this predicament? Sadly, quite easily. Despite the value I knew that meditation and other mindfulness practices held for me, I'd let them slip by the wayside because there was just *so much going on*, and so much of it was so emotionally charged. Aside from this graduation, more family would soon be visiting, another son's wedding was coming up, and we were scheduled to host a large wedding recital dinner. Another son and his wife were also expecting their first child, and I'd been asked to be a labor coach in the delivery room. These were wonderful events, but so many big milestone moments piled one atop the other felt like a lot. And Past Shawna did not want to slow down and sit with that "a lot."

In trying to cope with all the stress, my successful new habits of mindfulness were thrown out the window as Past Shawna came rearing back in to run the show. I fell back into familiar, comfortable patterns because that was "easier" during this stressful time. Repetitive Bitch to the rescue! "We don't need to process all these big, scary emotions," she said. "Or ask for help. Pfft! We'll just do like we used to and worry about all these little details to the standard of sheer perfection instead, because that's what has always 'worked' and takes less conscious awareness and mental energy. After all, we have a ton of shit to do . . ."

That moment in the stands is not one I will ever forget. The following week, I reached out to a counselor and returned to my meditation practice. Thankfully, by the time the wedding and my grandchild's birth rolled around in September (a few days apart from each other, *eek*), I had put Past Shawna's harmful ways back in the bottle. I am not so arrogant to believe she is gone forever. She remains part of me, waiting to come back if my stress level strays too high and if I fail to notice her pushing to return. She did her best to serve me well for years, and, heck, she has accomplished some great things, but letting myself be driven by my subconscious thoughts and fears comes with too high a price to pay.

After all, I don't want to spend so much time worrying about the past or the future that I miss out on all the blessings occurring right under my nose, right in *this* moment.

Row *with* the Tide Instead of against It

So, here's something I've learned since that day in the stands: emotional responses to experiences are not selective.

You can't just turn off the negative ones and expect the awesome ones to come freely strolling in. That's just not how our minds seem to work. Mindfulness practices help us to be able to recognize and get comfortable with all those shifting and morphing emotional reactions and responses. This is key to learning to embrace peace and purpose and to create lasting change in our lives, because if we can't welcome—or at least learn to accept—all emotional experiences, then they can seem threatening, scary, and worth avoiding at all costs. Avoiding feeling those tough but normal emotional experiences can dampen *all* of our emotional reactions, including the ones that make life worth living. Practicing mindful awareness is the best way I've come across to prevent the hollow numbness I suffered in those graduation stands. Bottom line: Without mindfulness, we tend to go through the motions of our lives without understanding why we do the things we do. Not only that, but we also don't understand why we *don't* try the exciting things we know we could or why we continue to do the things we really need to stop. Mindfulness gives us the ability to understand all of this *without* harsh self-judgment. Once we truly understand the underlying reasons for why we're acting a certain way, we can then take whatever steps are needed to move forward.

In this chapter, we'll delve into mindfulness practices and how adopting them can help us to better understand our own thoughts, feelings, and behavior. We'll also look at how mindfulness affects our Inner Bitches, and I'll point you toward some specific types of mindfulness practices that you can try to see if they work for you.

First up, though, let's take a closer look at how being unaware of what's going on inside of us affects how we live our lives day to day.

How You *Think* You Feel Is Just the Tip of the Iceberg

Cognitive neuroscience estimates that only 5 percent of our decisions, emotions, and behavior is generated from conscious thought, leaving the remaining 95 percent to occur from the subconscious. And guess what? The thought patterns that tend to get us caught up, stuck, and not able to change are the subconscious ones—which many of us tend to be wholly unaware of.

As mentioned in the previous chapter, these subconscious thoughts, emotions, and decisions are further complicated by the fact that we all carry out our lives based on *perceptions* of our environment, as well as the people and the events in it. These perceptions are shaped and molded into views based on our past experiences, which means that many of the narratives playing out in our heads—without us even realizing they're there—were written for us and heavily imprinted on our learning and growing brains as kiddos. No matter how fabulous our parents were, none of us get out of childhood without some mixed-up messages being interpreted by our far-from-developed little brains. Those messages stick and turn into stories we believe to be true, not just about ourselves, but about the world around us, how it works, and our roles within it. These stories then go on to form the framework for not just our conscious opinions but also our subconscious thoughts, feelings, and ultimately behaviors, unless we become more self-aware.

All this stuff simmering below the surface is often what drives us to do or *not* do things. To follow fear's dictates or act courageously. To say yes or to say no. To take a chance or sit it out, even against what seems to be the obvious choice for our success or well-being. During my nursing career, I saw people with uncontrolled diabetes continue high-sugar eating patterns and lose lower limbs. They had been told for years that this was a likely outcome if they didn't change their behavior. But the siren song that Survival Bitch ("Life is tough right now. This will make me feel better!") and Repetitive Bitch ("We habited this because it keeps patching holes in our boat and we haven't figured out any other way to stop from sinking . . .") weave when they put their heads together is powerful and hard to deny. Bottom line, as long as the underlying need that caused the adoption of that no-longer-wanted behavior isn't recognized and met in a new and more constructive way, it can seem all but impossible to change.

Here is an example of my own underlying perception and need. In the past, I used to get into arguments with my husband over the smallest of things, like when he forgot to start the dishwasher or to get milk on the way home from work. Only later was I able to consciously see and give language to the fact that, for me, his forgetting things made me feel alone and on my own. Once I unpacked that and the roots of where that "alone" feeling came from (in part, I realized, from formative memories of sitting in the dentist's chair as a kid getting fillings without my parents present), I could finally communicate effectively with my husband about why sometimes those little things could seem so big to me. This allowed him to understand how important his remembering was to me and try to do better—but, more importantly, once I worked with my false story of solitude, I could clearly see that I certainly was *not* on my own. Even if my husband still forgets stuff on a regular basis, he is there by my side for so much more.

When we begin to fully see and understand these narratives in an open and compassionate way, then we can begin to not only think but *act* in ways that better serve our spirit in the moment. That, in a nutshell, is why mindfulness is the key to helping us find joy and create lasting positive change in our lives. Additionally, we should never forget or diminish the fact that looking deep within ourselves is where we find a great deal of life's magic and beauty. The subconscious often contains our most cherished and genuine hopes and dreams, which can be powerful and exhilarating forces with which to create change energy.

The Mindful Bitch in Action

Mindfulness is such a buzzword these days that it's important to understand what it actually means. One of my favorite definitions comes from Kristin Neff, who writes, "Mindfulness is a non-judgmental, receptive mind state in which one observes thoughts and feelings as they are, without trying to suppress or deny them." Studies show that mindfulness practices like meditation can reduce stress, foster greater peace and happiness, and even provide a powerful self-help tool for people with mood disorders like anxiety and depression.[10]

There are many ways to achieve this mind state. The trick is to find what works for you. Below, I'll be talking a lot about meditation because it is the single best method I've found yet to keep us mindful from day to day. But before we actually get to the methods aspect of all this, first we need to understand why mindfulness is important in the context of your Inner Bitches.

Remember, each of the Inner Bitches is a construct stand-in for a set of drives that exist in each one of us. All three are always at work within us, but without mindfulness, we are often unaware of their roles and what they are up to moment to moment, and we are perhaps even less aware of why they are doing it. In order to create lasting fundamental change in your life and become a truly Powerful Bitch, you first have to be able to tune in during your day and be aware of what those wonderful but wacky ladies who live inside you are up to.

An example might be that you are trying to figure out how to create a spreadsheet for a work project. Maybe this isn't one of your strengths, and you're starting to think, "Ugh. I am never going to figure this out." The thought activates Survival Bitch. Seeking to ease your distress, she wants you to stop what you're doing *right now*. Her yucky response often triggers you to experience additional stressful thoughts. "Welp. I just can't win." Your shoulders slump, and you think about giving up. The familiar negative response gets Repetitive Bitch invited to the party, and she says, "Time for a distraction. Ooh! I know, let's check out that shit show that was unraveling on social media this morning." *Aaaand* you're off. Not only do you get no further along with

10   Teresa M. Edenfield and Sy Atezaz Saeed, "An update on mindfulness meditation as a self-help treatment for anxiety and depression," *Psychology Research and Behavior Management* 5 (2012): 131–141, https://doi.org/10.2147/PRBM.S3493.

your challenging work task, but you don't feel any better at all when you finally return to that task.

So where might mindfulness come into play in this scenario? Let's say that instead of giving in to that negative thought loop and the sudden desire for distraction, you instead decided to notice what was playing out in your mind as a curious observer instead of being caught up in the middle of it. (It can help to imagine the cascade of your thoughts as a waterfall; instead of standing under them, in the middle of the deluge, you simply take two steps to the right, where you can watch the flow instead of standing in it.) You can learn to focus on the resulting sensations in the body and the cadence of the breath when certain thought content generates in the mind. And what if you did this while practicing some deep-breathing exercises to turn off fight-flight-freeze mode? Many of my clients first notice a tension between the shoulder blades and a tight feeling in their chests when they feel overwhelmed, alone, or incompetent. Sadness sometimes feels like an overall fatigue, but you can learn to differentiate between this kind of tired feeling versus the good kind of fatigue from a hard day of manual labor or a good workout. If you don't know how to pause and get in touch with what you're really experiencing using mindfulness, it becomes very hard to tell these two different types of fatigue apart, and you may not be able to respond appropriately. That applies equally for all feeling messages. They are trying to tell you something important.

This simple act of being aware of your thoughts and sensations while taking deep breaths will show you two important things. First, *you are not your thoughts or your feelings*. Their current content, whether negative, positive, or somewhere in between, does not define who you are at your core essence. The second thing it will show you is that you have power over your current situation, in how you choose to look at and be in it.

While being a curious observer of your thoughts, you can halt or slow their negative downward spiral. You can dial down that fight, flight, or freeze response and engage rest and digest mode. And you know what that means. That's right, Charge Bitch is back in the building, ready to offer her two cents on what might be the best way to handle this. Maybe she'll say, "Hey, kid! You have been working with no break for four hours now and are freakin' tired. How about we reassess our failures after a walk, a snack, or a nap?" or, "If you really can't figure this out, maybe we can ask Amanda to help. She has offered and is really good at these things."

The power of mindfulness is that it gives you the chance to witness that first unhelpful thought before it unravels into twenty or thirty more, not just ruining moments and hours but *days* of your life. It gives you the power to nip a small problem in the bud before it grows into a much bigger and more complicated problem.

Another consideration in this is that behavioral science often speaks of two types of coping mechanisms, differentiating between *problem-solving coping mechanisms* (i.e., Charge Bitch's role) *versus emotional-level coping mechanisms* (attending to the feelings and reactions). I believe both are needed to manage your life for maximum happiness and success. Either way, if you can learn to just detach a little from an uncomfortable experience you're having and foster Survival Bitch's return to calm, Charge Bitch's problem-solving is going to be a lot easier, clearer, and more likely to benefit all the Bitches in the long term.

Meditation

As I mentioned before, there are many different types of mindfulness practices. Some people like to practice expressive journaling every day, or go for long walks, and find they can best observe their thoughts through those practices. For me, though, and for the majority of my clients, we find that nothing beats meditation.

The reason for this is that meditation—a practice in every sense of the word—cultivates the kind of attention we're trying to achieve day in and day out to what is happening in the mind, the body, and often, notably, the breath. The more you practice paying attention to what is truly happening within yourself, the more the skill of awareness will be available for application whenever you need it—like when your boss drops a surprise project in your lap at three o'clock on a Friday, when you're already thinking about wine o'clock later with your girlfriends.

It's also important to frame your practice the right way. A meditative pause isn't just something you do "in the classroom," or in therapy, or on your couch while you're alone. It's something you can do darn near anywhere, at any time, as long as you can find a moment of quiet . . . even if that quiet only exists at the moment within yourself. It's also not something you do a few times and then are done with. "Well! That's that. I learned to meditate, and now I'm good." Nope. The benefits of this practice require that you continue doing just that— practicing. You're never *done* meditating or learning to be mindful because life, its distractions, and your thoughts about it never stop flowing. There will always be a need to be able to take a step back and observe so that you understand how best to respond, and there will always be rough edges of yourself that could use some fine-tuning in order to become more whole.

We cannot hope to change what we cannot view with clear eyes. Meditation gives us some space from our own circular thinking. We can watch, witness, and assess with open curiosity, which offers a less emotionally entangled and more open viewpoint.

From there, a whole new world of opportunities arises, providing you with extremely powerful choices going forward.

Okay, but How Do I Actually Do This?

If you shared my initial skepticism about all of this hippie-dippie meditation stuff but are now finding yourself interested in giving it a try, there is still the hurdle of figuring out what to actually *do*. The idea of meditation often conjures up images of solemn Buddhist monks contemplating the divine mysteries of the universe. *Whoa.* Intimidating much? It really doesn't have to be that complicated.

There are plenty of ways to meditate and practice mindfulness. For many years, I just sat and focused on my breath and listened to my kitchen clock tick. While doing this, I tried valiantly to switch my focus back and forth from my breath to the clock, over and over again. As I progressed further, I explored guided relaxation meditations, which I still find *hugely* helpful in my own practice.

Many of my clients enjoy apps like Headspace and Calm. UCLA has free guided meditations that are brief and novice-friendly, and YouTube has some powerful guided meditations for varying needs.

Transcendental meditation uses mantras. Mindvalley has an amazing blog with further resources and explanations.

Yoga can be another powerful form of meditation practice. Yoga Nidra is my new obsession and is usually done as a form of guided meditation that allows you to focus on sequential bodily sensations, oftentimes with some imagery. I often find myself arriving at that place somewhere between wakefulness and sleep with Yoga Nidra. To me, it feels somewhat reminiscent of riding in the back of a car as a child, where you felt the hum of the engine through the car seat and heard the sound of the tires on gravel and felt *almost* asleep.

There have been endless books written and talks given about how to meditate, so I won't attempt to give an exhaustive account of methods here. I will suggest, though, that you seek out what has been expertly and compassionately covered on this topic by mindfulness giants such as Jon Kabat-Zinn, Jack Kornfield, Pema Chödrön, Tara Brach, Eckhart Tolle, and Thích Nhât Hanh, to name just a few.

In my own meditation practice, I may find that I start losing focus with a thought about chores, then skip to the last conversation I had with a friend, and then end up thinking about how to solve a work issue. It is okay if this happens a lot in the beginning! Again, the goal is not to force your mind to stop thinking. The goal is to gently redirect it to your focus of choice and to commit to developing a regular meditation practice to strengthen your attention circuits. It doesn't matter if you need to refocus 3,000 times. You are literally making changes in your brain, and the strong pull of distraction will lessen with time. A regular meditation practice allows you to become adept at the wonderful skill of intentional focus. In study after study, it has been shown that, with practice, you will begin to experience a separation and witnessing of your thoughts and their resulting emotional reactions in your body.[11] This is often referred to as metacognitive awareness, something that every human on the planet can use to their benefit in all aspects of life.

After beginning with a practice of singular focus, one can expand to wider perspectives. Keep in mind that the body is a constant barometer of what is happening in your head and vice versa. Consider it fair warning that negative

11   Jonathan Gibson, "Mindfulness, Interoception, and the Body: A Contemporary Perspective," *Frontiers in Psychology* 10 (September 2019): https://doi.org/10.3389/fpsyg.2019.02012.

thought patterns enjoy being sticky and tend to try to pull us into the rabbit hole of even more unhelpful thinking. With practice, though, we are less likely to get caught in the vortex and take the bait, instead learning to merely observe the negative thoughts briefly and then return to a present-moment focus, such as the breath, a mantra, or a comfortable place in the body.

Deep practice involves staying with the tough emotional sensations instead of shutting them down or distracting yourself from them with internal stories or busyness. If you can learn to tolerate the discomfort of the sensations, even for a minute or two, you will gain huge insight into what happens when you just stay present a few seconds longer. This is often called "surfing the waves" because the uncomfortable sensations may crescendo briefly, but perhaps then they will lighten or change quality. Frequently, what happens next is the sensations will paradoxically pass.

Whatever is there is okay. It will come and go, as it always has. The only difference will be how you relate to it, your response. In the end, that is the greatest power you can have. Eventually, the difference will be you. One of the worst things about experiencing the effects that accompany anxiety and depression is hopelessness in the belief that your feelings are something you will never be equipped to handle, or that they will remain a permanently intolerable state. Mindfulness offers the crucial lesson that, eventually, all things change, even the thoughts in your head and the feelings in your body. And the experience of uncomfortable thoughts and feelings is made much easier when you show yourself how to be with them using a self-compassionate form of attention.

All of these advanced levels of mindfulness practices use your focus and attention skills to witness your own thoughts and feelings and clearly view all your Inner Bitches in action. Making choices with this deeper self-understanding combined with a healthy respect for physiological needs offers the complete behavior and mindset change needed for permanent transformation—the kind of transformation needed on the path to peace and purpose.

Being Present

Developing a practice of mindfulness like meditation brings important new insights—not just about what we think and feel, but about our sometimes-confusing reactions to the events and situations in our lives. But just because you acknowledge what is already there doesn't mean you have to act on it right away—you're simply witnessing what is present with newfound clarity and perspective. The beauty of mindfulness is that it offers a space to adjust to some internal rumblings and familiarize yourself with your automatic responses (i.e., the workings of your Inner Bitches) and how they may arrive in varying circumstances so that you know yourself better and can respond as needed in the moment, and in perhaps new ways . . . right Bitch, right response, right time.

For instance, imagine that you feel unhappy in your marriage, but you realize you've been denying this truth to yourself and others. Acknowledging the loneliness or sadness doesn't mean you have to file for divorce today, but it does give you the opportunity to observe the changes in your experiences within the marriage. Do things change when you have couple time, or when you are getting time for self-care? What about when he helps out, or when you thank him for the contributions he makes, or when he has your back with your mother-in-law? Did something change when one of you switched jobs? Observation offers wisdom, options for active solutions to any problems you may be having, and a greater sense of control and calm while you address them.

Also, please be oh so kind to yourself if you're struggling with starting your practice because you worry the cascade of emotions will be too overwhelming or won't ever stop. Remember: The pace is yours to set. This is dipping your toe in the water. Your show, your time. If you do begin and it is too much, stop, and, when in doubt, please seek outside counsel if the symptoms you are experiencing from facing tough things are affecting your quality of life. Some traumas, obviously, must first be unearthed with the guidance of a professional.

Until we live in the gray, we cannot imagine the gray. As a recovering perfectionist, I found that seeing my over-the-top, over-doing behaviors was painful because I was convinced if I stopped the performance, everything in my world would fall apart. I would fail to pay the bills, feed the kids, show up to work, and remain a functioning part of society. You get it, total Armageddon. You may laugh, but there has to be some deep reason for never going to bed with dirty dishes in the sink, don't ya think?

I know it is hard. Repetitive Bitch is always pulling for things to stay the same, and Survival Bitch gets irked with change. But change is what you are hoping for, right?

Meditation and other mindfulness techniques, talk therapy, and expressive journaling are good places to begin mindful permanent change. I don't care if insight arrives at your doorstep in the form of transcendental mantras, Yoga Nidra, loving-kindness meditation, body scanning meditation, staring at a candle flame, or simply focusing on the sensation of your right pinkie toe. If you are intent on the practice, it will expand out to the rest of your life. You will catch yourself examining your kids' cute dimples, listening to sounds in the forest, and, yes, noticing subconscious thoughts of impending doom as they pop up inexplicably—in time to prevent them from turning your pleasant day into a scene from *Mad Max: Fury Road*.

In order to rewrite your story so that it stars your most brilliant self, *you've got to first know the original one.* We can't just expect Charge Bitch to be able to run the show on knowledge and willpower alone (more on that in the next chapter). We complex, emotionally driven, beautiful creatures make many of our decisions based on emotions and often-unconscious beliefs and perceptions. If you don't know the original story that Survival Bitch is operating under and you keep trying to force a new set of rules for living with knowledge and willpower alone, real change can seem elusive and insurmountable.

With mindfulness techniques, you will be able to clearly identify what this unfolding inner drama truly represents. Your gaining insight into who you are and what you truly want will offer an inner confidence like you have never known. With practice, we begin to unhook old life stories, heal relationships, and have courageous conversations. We possess more comfort in our own skin. We are freer to pursue scary goals and feel deserving when we achieve them. And we prepare to embark on this journey with a new appreciation for being kind to ourselves.

In the next chapter, we'll take a closer look at the role self-compassion plays in finding peace and joy and creating long-lasting positive change.

After all, even the most Powerful Bitches need kindness.

CHAPTER FIVE:

SELF-COMPASSION: HEALING SURVIVAL BITCH

"If your compassion does not include yourself, it is incomplete."
—Jack Kornfield, *Buddha's Little Instruction Book*

Survival Bitch Snuggling

Encountering an area of self-improvement more poorly understood than self-compassion is pretty rare. We're talking "winning big on the ten dollars' worth of scratch-off tickets your mother-in-law gave you for Christmas again this year" rare. Just raising this subject in group settings results in uncomfortable seat-shifting and broken eye contact to a greater degree than asking your teenage boy why your "we think you might like" streaming suggestions have suddenly become more than a little risqué.

That's because the entire concept of self-compassion is largely misunderstood.

Let's back up a moment to explore why this might be. Many of us assume the road to success is a trail blazed by pushing ourselves to the limit, trying longer and harder, and shaming ourselves into a full-on embrace of hustle culture. Remember those internal narratives we talked about previously? The ones that take hold when we're young and go on to shape our worldviews? Well, part of the internal narrative of many of us who grew up in America is that our self-worth is intrinsically tied to how productive we are and how many outside trappings of material success we have acquired. In light of this internal script, acts of self-compassion are often viewed as quitting, excuse-giving, or—*gasp!*— admitting weakness.

Did you feel yourself shrink back right there? If you did, you're not alone.

While our young brains are developing, we can't help but receive or interpret messages from the adults around us of worthiness or unworthiness in response to pretty much everything we do. And while the criteria our wee young noggins use to determine whether a behavior we exhibited is "good" (makes us feel worthy) or "bad" (makes us feel unworthy) might seem nonsensical to use today as adults, it persists nonetheless.

For example, let's say at age eleven, you agreed to someone else's plans without voicing your own differing preferences. That someone said, "You are just so sweet." Survival Bitch felt really secure in that moment. Big tribal acceptance! Her survival brain experienced a positive rush of hormones and brain chemicals, which led to the natural desire to remember everything about the details of the scenario to be able to repeat it again in the future—over and over again. So she does, which leads to Repetitive Bitch solidifying this routine into efficient, low-energy, nicely laid down tracks. This turned into a mighty strong people-pleasing habit and now, thirty years later, you find yourself instinctually agreeing to what other people want you to do with or for them, whether you actually want to do the thing they asked you to or not. As soon as they leave the room, you face-palm and ask yourself, "Oh my god, why did I agree to this crap again?!" But it's just so freakin' hard to say no . . . because Survival Bitch and Repetitive Bitch literally wired your brain to do this automatically.

As we've discussed, these kinds of events often occur before the most evolved parts of our brains are fully developed, or, if they occur during adulthood, in situations of intense emotional impact. Therefore, these messages (the sense of which may have gotten pretty garbled along the way) were stored as upmost priority in Survival Bitch's mind.

Remember, one of Survival Bitch's primary purposes is to help you develop skills to prevent or *cope* with anything in life that could cause you harm, often engaging your fight-flight-freeze response—whether what she is responding to is actual life-threatening danger or just dealing with the difficult issues of things like unresolved trauma or stress surges from work or relationship strains. These coping skills serve a purpose. Yes, eating Doritos every night was a skill that allowed you to cope. Shutting down and going to bed was a skill that allowed you to cope. How can you be angry with that? You survived.

The kicker is now you've decided that some of the Survival Bitch coping skills that once helped you are no longer serving you. They may even be causing you harm.

So what's the best way to let them go gracefully and adopt long-lasting positive change? As you might have guessed from the title of this chapter, self-compassion plays a big role here. But why is that?

Stop Beating Yourself Up . . . No, *Really!*

I am about to drop some life-changing knowledge on you. Are you ready?

Here goes.

You can't self-flagellate, shame, or bully yourself into change. It just does not work—not permanently, anyway. Change requires you to look upon your own flawed self with acceptance, empathy, and love. In a nutshell, it requires self-compassion.

We're going to explore multiple aspects of what self-compassion means throughout this chapter, but the first definition I want you to hear—deep in your soul—is this: self-compassion means learning to love Survival Bitch and everything she has taught you, even the bits that don't serve you anymore. Even if they hurt more than help now, there was a point in your life (maybe even years and years) when you needed those warning systems and coping strategies to get through something really difficult. It's important to honor that. When we don't, we create shame, and shame creates shrinking back and a sense of unworthiness—a far cry from the state required to change and become powerful.

In order to create long-lasting positive change in your life and let go of coping skills and strategies that aren't helpful any longer, you first need to be able to take a long, hard look at Survival Bitch's fears and inadequacies and be able to view them (and her) with love and understanding. Until she receives proper attention, she will continue to cloud clarity on what you want and deserve and therefore impact your ability to become a Powerful Bitch. After all, as long as Survival Bitch feels unheard and is still in pain, she's going to push to continue those now-problematic coping skills. Failing to show ourselves compassion makes us feel more unhappy, more frustrated, and more stuck in the negative feedback loop of bad feelings spurring bad habits that create still more bad feelings. Rinse, recycle, repeat.

On the flip side, learning to be more self-compassionate comes with a host of benefits. It leads to improvements in our relationships. It allows us to experience less dissatisfaction with our bodies and less rumination over past events. Self-compassion fosters a more positive state of mind with greater curiosity and optimism, allowing us to see and seize new possibilities and opportunities. Self-compassionate people worry less about failure, so they take chances and try new things. And if they don't succeed, they are much more likely to try, try again. They also tend to have much better self-care habits—like getting adequate sleep and exercise and keeping up with preventive health-care checks. Most importantly, perhaps, people who practice regular self-compassion are more resilient when they encounter adversity, and they experience life as being more joyful.

In this chapter, we'll learn the three tenets of authentic self-compassion so that you can put them into practice. We'll also discuss the difference between self-compassion and self-pity and talk about how to avoid setting ourselves up to fail with unrealistic expectations when we seek to create sweeping changes in our lives using only knowledge and willpower.

The Three Tenets of Self-Compassion

Self-compassion offers a gentler approach to self-discovery without subjecting ourselves to all the usual harsh internal judgments. Many of us find ourselves in the position of needing change. However, without an awareness of what already exists that is keeping us stuck, we find it almost impossible to move forward with any serious traction.

As we seek to practice self-compassion while we move toward positive change in our lives, the framework created by noted self-compassion expert Dr. Kristin Neff is a useful tool in changing the way we think about how we ought to treat ourselves. (If you haven't read her best-selling book *Self-Compassion: The Proven Power of Being Kind to Yourself*, I highly recommend it.)

Dr. Neff proposes three key components of what it means to be truly self-compassionate:

1. Self-Kindness versus Self Judgment
2. Mindfulness versus Overidentification
3. Common Humanity versus Isolation

Below, I share my take on these core tenets.

Self-Kindness versus Self-Judgment

One of the more common things we offer ourselves instead of kindness is self-judgment. But what does this self-judgment look like in practice?

It looks like telling yourself to "just get over it" when your friend cancels plans you made at the last minute again—after all, you *should* feel lucky to have her as a friend. It looks like feeling a little down for no special reason but telling yourself what you *should* feel is grateful—after all, you have a nice warm house, a good job, and your health. Self-judgment can also look like finding yourself in a place where you are unable to stop crying because your dog died, but instead of offering self-kindness, you tell yourself you are being ridiculous and "it's time to 'grow up,' it's been two months." Or maybe you screwed up an important email related to a job prospect and proceed to berate yourself for the next two weeks.

All of these are examples of moments where what you needed was a bit of kind acceptance and regard for your authentic feelings, but what you gave yourself instead was a dismissal or labeling of your feelings as childish, silly, or inappropriate.

It's helpful to curate positive thinking and gratitude, but oftentimes what you really need *first* is a hug, or just to do something nice for yourself as a way of acknowledging that you're actually having a hard time in the moment . . . and that's okay.

Each of us must find ways to lighten up on being our own worst critic and judging ourselves for what amounts to normal human experiences. Everyone feels sad or disappointed sometimes, and everyone makes mistakes. Expecting anything different from ourselves isn't even realistic, let alone kind.

It's okay to take a little time out for self-nurturing through experiences that leave us feeling a lack of confidence, connection, safety, or belonging. If we can ditch the shame and process kindly, *then* we can step back a bit and use Charge Bitch's intellect to choose actions that meet our needs wisely.

If you find yourself yelling, maybe you're not feeling heard, or maybe you feel lonely inside a relationship or unfulfilled in your career. The emotions you feel in these situations and the coping mechanisms you rely on are best regarded as signposts that something requires A) your attention and B) truly effective responses to whatever is actually wrong. Once that self-comforting attention is given, the pain diminishes, and healing can begin. Charge Bitch can offer input and strategize plans for resolution *if* needed.

On the other hand, if you merely judge, shove down, minimize, or avoid the issue, then the pain is more likely to fester and grow.

Instead, offer yourself a little compassion. Sometimes that simple acknowledgment that things are difficult is a huge help. Learn to say to yourself, "This load is heavy. This is hard." If it feels right, place a gentle hand on your heart.

When you speak to yourself with kindness, you activate "rest and digest" and clear the mind. Sometimes this simple act of self-soothing is all that is needed. If that's not the case, then at least Charge Bitch is back in the room and able to offer her valuable input.

Common Humanity versus Isolation

Human suffering is always made worse when we believe we are unique and alone in its experience. We often carry the false narrative that our suffering reflects our own shortcomings, forgetting that others face similar difficulties and that some suffering is inherent when living a full textured life.

It is an act of self-kindness to remember that we are not alone in struggling with heartbreak, hardship, and pain. We can alleviate our burden by reaching out to others with similar stories. Commonality can be found by researching blogs and forums or even watching movies or reading great works of literature (even a fictional character's struggle can make you feel less alone). Support groups can also do wonders to ease the sense of isolation. While the story you find may not mirror the exact same circumstance you're dealing with, the common thread of being like all humans that sometimes suffer fosters a sense of collective and community.

Another area where we can misinterpret hard emotions is when we regularly assign negative mood states to character faults while attributing happiness and joy to outside circumstances. Think about it: "I am sad and tired again: What is wrong with me? Why am I so ungrateful and miserable?" versus "I am in a great mood today!"

"Why?" someone asks.

"Well, a friend did something kind." Or "I have a fun event coming up!" Or maybe just "Because it is Friday, silly."

Many of the women I coach struggle with speaking up and self-advocating and are frustrated with themselves for not being able to stop the fallout and ramifications for apparent complacency when they remain silent. Many were taught young that being a "good" girl meant being quiet, following rules imposed by others, and being accommodating. It can be hard to go against this unless you can see the origins of these beliefs clearly and how they may have become ingrained patterns. As women, many of us share a sisterhood in this struggle.

If you look around, you'll see pretty quickly that we all have broken pieces, insecurities, and low moments. Isolation and separation add further to this suffering. Learning to see our similarities in this goes so far in easing the burden.

Mindfulness versus Overidentification

Another way we can practice self-kindness and compassion is to lovingly watch for when we may fall into the trap of overidentifying with our thoughts and emotions. I talked about this a good deal in the Mindfulness chapter, but it's worth repeating here: *you* are not your thoughts or your emotional responses to them. It's helpful to remember that they are produced by biochemical reactions to what the brain perceives is happening or likely to happen based on past experiences.

Again, these are mere reflections of our perceptions of the moment-to-moment experiences we are having and can vary greatly by so many factors in life. Shaming ourselves about what we feel never helps resolve life's difficulties. When we doubt and berate ourselves for tough but normal human reactions, we only ensure they will stay around longer and cause more suffering. A Buddhist parable describes this self-flagellation as "the second arrow." In a nutshell, shit happens and then we blame and judge ourselves for being hurt and the pain worsens tenfold.

Becoming familiar with your own inner workings gives you power because you become intimately knowledgeable around what situations, people, and activities energize you and which ones leave you feeling drained. Lean into your favorite mindfulness practice(s) with an open curiosity and working with *all* emotional reactions will seem less daunting, I swear.

Battling Judgment and Unrealistic Expectations: Why Knowledge and Willpower Alone Aren't Enough to Create Change

We have spent a fair amount of time here discussing how failure to acknowledge Survival Bitch's current or past pain leads to the inability to create lasting positive change in our lives. I think it's also worth mentioning here that this failure itself can lead to a lot of unhelpful self-judgment. A common mis-conception I see with clients is that they expect themselves to be able to foster big changes in their lives on knowledge and willpower alone, but, as you might now be beginning to understand, a more "whole Bitch" approach is needed.

Don't get me wrong, knowledge and willpower are *great*. Both are helpful when trying to create change, but they're not enough on their *own* to power you through it. We've established that we can't create true change without learning to observe Survival Bitch in action and to treat her with some love, respect, and kindness via self-compassion.

So, what's the issue with willpower and knowledge? Well, for starters, they exist squarely in Charge Bitch's territory.

I am sure you have experienced the futility of trying to use logic to heal old wounds or rewrite old stories. There's Charge Bitch with all her precisely laid out statistics, facts, and figures, case citing repeatedly why you should be "over it." And yet, it has been *decades,* and your pain stays the same. So . . . maybe we can begin to accept that her reasoning may not be the healing balm we all need.

Below, let's take a closer look at some of the pitfalls we encounter when we assume that willpower and knowledge alone are enough to create lasting change.

Willpower

Women label themselves as lacking willpower like that's a character flaw. It's not. A lack of willpower often reflects not yet finding the authentic moti-vation, support, or confidence needed to follow through with a plan. Some-times the plans themselves rely solely on willpower, and these are bound to fail because A) willpower is not always easily accessible and B) willpower is not limitless.

Think of your daily allotment of willpower as a bank account you withdraw money from *all day long*. After all, willpower is used in your thought process for most decisions you make, because it's what allows you to curb your own behavior (another of Charge Bitch's functions) and do what you know you need to do to stay on-task and on-plan. It's what you use to get up and go to work in the morning, and to resist the urge to flip off your boss when she zings you with a backhanded compliment, and for a million and one other split-second choices you make all day long, every day.

We know that Charge Bitch is phenomenal (and so smart!), but she, too, has her limits. The self-care "platform" habits we learned in chapter 2 (especially exercise) potentiate willpower and help keep Charge Bitch functioning well enough to access the wisdom required to make the best long-term choices. But even with a great self-care routine in place, Charge Bitch will eventually deplete her in-the-moment willpower stores and decisional bucks for the day and get tired. And when that happens, one or both of the other two Bitches have got to take the wheel. Shocker, they often don't have the same destination in mind as Charge Bitch. In fact, they can most often be found cruising toward Easy Funtown, USA, with the sunroof open and your favorite song blasting.

Bottom line: Expecting Survival Bitch and Repetitive Bitch to employ willpower is like leaving your nine-year-old child alone in an ice cream factory for an hour and expecting them to walk away without a tummy ache. It's just not going to happen.

That's why expecting to power through big changes in your life on willpower alone just isn't going to cut it. It is an act of considerable self-compassion to recognize this, because then you can finally stop judging and blaming yourself for not having enough of something you're not actually *built* to have a limitless supply of every minute of every day. In the next chapter, we will talk about how to set yourself up to rely *less* on willpower in your quest for change.

Knowledge

Like willpower, working knowledge is Charge Bitch's turf. But, as I'm sure you're all too aware at this point in your life, just because Charge Bitch logically knows something to be the soundest course of action for your life, your relationship, and/or your health doesn't mean you will automatically do that thing.

If only it were that easy, right?

The simple truth is that knowledge isn't enough to power us through big changes either. Charge Bitch can dive whole hog into all of the books, podcasts, Facebook groups, documentaries, government websites, and expert consultations needed to research a topic down to its nitty-gritty, most finite details. But at the end of the day, knowledge does not equal action, so it cannot commute itself into change—not on its own. I like to tell my clients, "Knowledge is an *opportunity* for change, but it is not the change itself."

A good way to test this theory is to create a pros and cons list related to making one healthy change you'd like to implement in your life. Now, you're going to make this list using *only* Charge Bitch's logic and learned knowledge. I bet the con side is very light, right? And the pros side has some real heavy hitters. For instance, if you're trying to quit smoking, on the pros side is "Cigarettes cause fatal lung disease and cancer and can decrease fertility. Quitting smoking will substantially cut my risk of these things." You know this, so why is quitting so dang hard to do?

Ah, you see, our exercise is not done yet. Now make a new list for the same life change using Survival Bitch's opinions instead. Be real with yourself. How does *she* truly feel about giving up something or beginning a change routine? Yeah, it's likely going to look *very* different.

The truth is that smoking or drinking or eating or gambling, or whatever habit Charge Bitch logically decided is no longer working for you, serves a need: for stress management, for fun, for love and connection, and a host of other possibilities. Until you acknowledge and replace the need, knowledge alone is just not enough. When you're trying to implement a change in your life, you first need to understand how Survival Bitch feels about the new plan and find a way to convince her it's A) rewarding and B) doesn't go against her understandable inclination to seek safety and comfort.

Bottom line: Stop punishing yourself for knowing better. After all, that's a start, but it's not even half the battle.

Self-Compassion Is Not the Same Thing as Self-Pity

Now, before you begin to imagine that using self-compassion will result in you becoming a complacent slug, please understand that self-compassionate people still value working toward the best versions of themselves, now and in the future. They still make hard choices and value actions of self-care. The advantage they have is that they've learned to skip the exhausting extra step of adding additional and unnecessary suffering that occurs when one beats oneself up for the mistakes, moods, and pitfalls inherent in living a complicated human life.

Self-compassion does not mean feeling sorry for yourself, and it's not a free pass to throw yourself a nonstop pity party. The key difference here is that self-compassion comforts, uplifts, and empowers us, while self-pity *disempowers* us.

For example, say you didn't get the job you applied for. You're disappointed. Somehow, this becomes a key example supporting a story you believe to be true about yourself: "Nothing ever works out for me." You spend weeks on the couch feeling helpless, complaining to friends and family, eating comfort food. These are acts of self-pity.

Self-compassion is different. When we act self-compassionately, we recognize the stories playing out in our heads that lead us to believe things like "nothing ever works out for me." But instead of allowing ourselves to accept those stories as true, we acknowledge that they are stories we *used* to believe, and they caused further pain. We can relabel the feelings associated with not getting the job as the normal human reaction of disappointment.

The next time you feel disappointed, try doing what we talked about earlier. Place that hand over your heart and offer yourself a little compassion. Say, "It's okay that you're a little sad." Breathe into it and take care of yourself. It's amazing what even a simple, kind, self-directed gesture can do. When we perform small acts of self-kindness when we are hurting or disappointed, the weight seems to lift, and we are more likely to bounce back and try again. Self-pity? Me think not.

The key difference is that self-compassion acknowledges that life can be hard sometimes, but this is not the same as excuse-making. It is simply allowing for the irrefutable inevitability of screwing up or being less than perfect sometimes. As a result, we are able to learn from our mistakes and actually *work* to prevent them from being repeated.

Excuses work differently. They rarely lead to taking positive action, like offering a sincere apology or acknowledging our less-than-optimal reaction to a situation and committing to doing differently the next time after we've made a mistake. I am a great example of this when I don't give myself breaks or make time in my life for fun. Irritability is my warning signal, and sometimes I am too late in noticing its presence before someone else is affected. Self-compassion doesn't mean not apologizing; it means looking at the circumstances that led to the outburst, offering self-compassion, making a plan, following through with needed changes, *and* apologizing. Accountability and responsibility can be intertwined with self-compassion. They are not mutually exclusive.

Self-pity and shame turn us inward, while true self-compassion fosters positive action and addressing core issues. That is an excellent barometer to use if you're ever in doubt about which is which.

Fill the Well

The benefits of self-compassion don't stop at your own door. Empathy for others becomes more readily available when we can tune into ourselves and acknowledge and soothe our own suffering. Each act of self-compassion helps us to recognize the suffering of others around us. Conversely, when we do not cut ourselves any slack, we don't cut much for others either, closing ourselves off not just from our own struggles, but from the struggles of those around us.

Just think about how pushing yourself to plow through a bunch of chores with a splitting headache can dim or completely extinguish any chance that you'll offer a kind response when your significant other arrives home from work and innocently mentions that it was a bitch of a day. Charge Bitch knows that saying, "Sorry, hon. It hasn't been fab for me either. Why don't we veg out and watch a movie tonight?" is a smart choice to make. But Survival Bitch is hurting, and you ignored it and now, without the pause of self-compassion, she might just come out with something along the lines of "Are you freaking kidding me? Let me tell you something . . ."

Now that you're learning more about the origin of Survival Bitch's perceptions and pain, my hope is that you will become able to recognize that her occasional less-than-ideal responses and patterns exist because she's legitimately trying to help you. Once you realize this, you can begin to approach that part of yourself with more kindness and understanding and find a path to healing and deeply rooted change.

Like Survival Bitch, Repetitive Bitch has a tendency to lock us into patterns and routines using her own particular superpower: the creation and maintenance of habits. Some habits are fantastic, while others . . . a little less so. In the next chapter, we'll take a look at how Repetitive Bitch functions and how to use her powers for the forces of good and not "aw, crap, I did it again."

CHAPTER SIX:

HIJACK YOUR OWN HABITS: HOW TO REWIRE REPETITIVE BITCH FOR WINNING

"All of life is an experiment.
The more experiments you make the better."
— Ralph Waldo Emerson

I'm Stuck on You

Breaking old habits is hard.

Just like any real-world path that is worn, a well-worn neuronal-grooved brain path is faster and easier to travel. Because our bodies are always aiming to conserve energy for survival purposes, our existing habits are the preferred route of choice. Old habits have also already been proven to be "safe," because we have done them a million times and here we are, still breathing. Many of these old Repetitive Bitch habits that we want to give up were formed to assist Survival Bitch in feeling rewarded or comforted, or they offered a sense of belonging. But now we've decided those behaviors are causing more harm than good, and we want to change them.

The trick is to not just change the habit itself, but to identify the need *behind* the habit so you can find a way to fill that need in a new and more effective manner. It's also important to do this using the self-compassion tools we covered in the last chapter.

Something I helped one of my clients—we'll call her Betsy—work through comes to mind as a good example. One of Betsy's happiest childhood memories was going for a ride in the car with her parents on Sunday afternoons. They'd run errands as a family and then finish up with a stop at their favorite neighborhood ice cream shop. Thus began a lifelong love of that sweet, cold, creamy goodness.

Once Betsy had a family of her own, she decided to carry on this tradition with her kids. Not surprisingly, her two kiddos came to look forward to ice cream Sundays just as much as Betsy had when she was their age.

Sounds wonderful, right? Unfortunately, in this case, there was a problem.

Like many folks, Betsy found herself dealing with unwanted weight gain, especially in the summer—prime ice cream season. When she first came to see me, she was having a terrible time dropping that extra fifteen pounds, a dilemma complicated by not wanting to give up those beloved ice cream Sundays with her kids. While working together on this issue, we two intrepid Inner Bitch detectives noticed a few useful tidbits of information. First, we went back to those early Sundays in her childhood and talked about how, over time, she'd come to identify eating ice cream as a source of comfort. Because of this, even years later as an adult, every time she ate ice cream, that sweet, cold stuff tapped right into all those warm and cozy feelings associated with the best parts of the bond she shared with her parents as a child. In other words, Survival Bitch had identified ice cream as a go-to source for meeting the normal need of self-soothing.

The second thing we uncovered together in our sleuthing was that, later in her life, Betsy found herself dealing with periods of depression. During the time when her depression reared its head, she developed a habit of numbing that pain with ice cream. Those occasions added up. Remember, when Survival Bitch notices that a particular behavior is effective in filling a need, it is repeated enough to become Repetitive Bitch habit territory. Once we perform it enough times, eventually, when a need arises, say, for comfort or calming down uncomfortable stress symptoms, those negative feelings in themselves become the cue to perform the habit. Achy feeling in the chest? Ice cream. Tense shoulders? Wine. Frustrated? Crunchy chips. At that point, the habit occurs rapidly without Charge Bitch having time to have input, which, in the immediate, is efficient, allowing her to avoid thinking, decision-making, and energy exertion. Unfortunately, when the crisis has passed, she often regrets the old habit routine and commits to do "better" the next time . . . *Shit.*

So, when Betsy felt low, she found herself falling into the habit of eating ice cream to feel better. It worked, in the short term at least, to ease her distress. But it added to her weight gain, which over time made her feel *more* depressed, not solely because of the weight but because it made her feel helpless in her ability to make changes.

You see where I'm going with this?

Sometimes certain habits get wired in and end up actually making the original problem our Inner Bitches were trying to deal with *worse*, not better, over the long term, even if the coping habit offers temporary relief. This can lead to a vicious cycle of repeating those habits and feeling stuck in a miserable unending loop, unable to achieve the positive changes we seek to create in our lives.

And that sucks.

Creating *Real* Change

The good news is this: Just as it's our Inner Bitches who get us into these kinds of messes, it's those same wacky broads who can get us out. The trick is to learn to notice what it is Survival Bitch is actually *getting* from an unwanted habit. Then you can find a good work-around to rewire in a replacement habit.

I won't pretend this is easy, but it is 100 percent achievable. It's a heckin' lot harder, though, if you try to rewire an unwanted habit *without* working with your Inner Bitches. If you try this without first getting Survival Bitch's buy-in, for instance, you'll likely return to the old habit because it was meeting a need. If you don't acknowledge that Charge Bitch has limitations, you may try to force overnight change with willpower and white-knuckle force alone, and we know how quickly that goes off track.

Repetitive Bitch is a habits prodigy when it comes to getting things done quickly and efficiently, including meeting many of those immediately pressing needs. You just have to learn how she operates. In the short term, being able to rewire your habits with the help of your Inner Bitches can improve your health and help you attain mastery over a whole host of things that are currently ailing you. In the long-term, seeing that you *can* change habits when needed meets your very human need for competency and agency over your life.

In the example above with Betsy, we used a twofold approach to achieve the change she sought.

The first part of our approach was acknowledging that she still needed a healthy way of self-soothing (but one that wasn't loaded with regret). Stress management and meditation became huge for her, as did flavored teas that she intentionally savored. In the evening, when ice cream was likely to beckon, she would treat herself to a slow foot rub with her favorite lotion while she called a friend or her mom. We also decided that what she was really getting out of ice cream Sundays with her kids was time to connect with them and that she shouldn't have to give up that beloved tradition.

To produce that same feeling of connection she got with her kids during the ice cream outings, we planned for her to have an enjoyable beverage instead and ask her kids a series of fun questions while *they* ate their ice cream. She is a brilliant journalist, so this was easy for her to do. Once she implemented these changes, Betsy found that she still got that sense of connection with her loved ones she'd been craving, and she didn't have to give up her family tradition with her kids—she just changed it a little. After gaining a greater familiarity with herself and her needs over time, she was able to return to enjoying ice cream during social events, but she did not return to using it as a self-soothing tool in low times. Win-win.

In this chapter, we'll learn the nuts and bolts of how habits work. We'll also talk more about the roles Survival Bitch and Repetitive Bitch play in the creation and maintenance of habits and how to use Charge Bitch to plan new ones. Equipped with this knowledge, you'll be starting from a much stronger foundation as you seek to identify and change any unwanted habits you may have. I'll also offer you some helpful tools and ideas to make it easier for you to rewire Repetitive Bitch, using her superpowers for the forces of awesome. Once you learn to realign your habits to meet Survival Bitch's emotional needs and Charge Bitch's energy requirements, you'll be well on your way to becoming the Powerful Bitch of your dreams.

First on the list: let's take a closer look at why we need Survival Bitch's buy-in when we're trying to change a habit.

Let's Review: Getting Survival Bitch on Board

So, as we've established, one of the main places where women go wrong when trying to drop unwanted habits and create better new ones is that we leave Survival Bitch completely out of the equation. The reason this doesn't work is that Survival Bitch is always going to be taking her turn at the wheel in making choices at various points throughout your day. Remember, Survival Bitch's needs for safety and rewards are *huge*. Secondly, willpower is what Charge Bitch wields like Excalibur in the face of all the things that try to get between you and your goals—but eventually she's going to conk out and leave Repetitive Bitch and Survival Bitch steering the ship.

That means any new habit or routine you're trying to cement in needs Survival Bitch's buy-in. If you fail to get her on board with your new habit, she's going to arrive home after a long week at work and laugh in the face of all those leafy greens and lean proteins stocked in the fridge while speed-dialing your favorite pizza joint around the corner. You have to think about change in terms of this: What is the *upside* for Survival Bitch? Get into the weeds on this for a moment.

Now, Survival Bitch prefers evidence of the existence of said upside via the feeling of being rewarded. Unfortunately, that "reward" feeling doesn't often come until after she has done the thing you're trying to talk her into doing—the thing she doesn't want to do. After all, getting up at six o'clock in the morning to work out sounds like it's going to make her feel like shit. And at first, *it can* . . . until one day soon, she notices less anxiety and clearer thinking at work on days when she has stuck to the new routine.

The trick is getting her started in earnest in the first place, and sometimes we have to build in temporary rewards to get her to stick with the new habit behavior long enough for the long-lasting benefits to kick in. We're going to talk about this in more depth below, but it's important to bear in mind Survival Bitch's role in the creation of new habits as we launch into what's up next: How do habits even work, in terms of how our brains work?

The Neuroscience of Habits

Let's talk expectations. Getting Repetitive Bitch to wire in a new habit doesn't happen overnight. Below, I'm going to walk you through the series of steps that make up this process. To begin, it will help if you think of this process less as *stopping* a habit, and more as *replacing* an old habit with a new one. It will also help, as you read through this next section, if you first identify a routine, habit, or repeated behavior—even just a pattern of thinking—in your own life that you'd like to replace with something better. If you need to, take a few moments now to think about this. It's going to help you to better absorb the new information you're about to learn, because you'll be able to think about how you might start to apply it immediately in your own life. I'll also be asking you to refer to this change you'd like to make and think through different aspects of it throughout the rest of this chapter.

After all, the goal here isn't just to read this book and be done. The goal is to start taking action toward becoming a Powerful Bitch. Replacing habits that no longer serve you with new and improved ones is one small step for woman, and one giant leap for Powerful Bitch-kind.

Step One: Identify the Cue

So, once you've identified what habit it is you'd like to change, the first step toward doing so is to determine what it is that triggers this unwanted habit into motion. What is the initial cue that gets the ball rolling on the behavior you want to quit or replace?

Here are some questions you can ask yourself to get started.

First off, is there a certain time of day when the habit occurs? If the answer is yes, start thinking through what is going on with your mind and body at that time. As simplistic as it sounds, is it a time of day when you are likely to be hungry or thirsty? Or tired? Or lonely? Or bored?

The people around you can also act as cues. For instance, maybe you have friends who love margaritas and want you to join in or coworkers who drag you down lamenting all day about how impossible they think it will be for any of you to find time to tackle the extra assignments required to move vertically in your company. Is the influence exerted on you by others in your environment preventing you from getting excited about starting new projects or setting new goals?

The cue could also come in the form of a certain type of interaction you experience, perhaps a "feelings hangover" from key individuals in your life.

In any case, look for patterns associated with your habit triggering. The cue can be physical or emotional, and it can be within you or something external from your surroundings. For example, clutter can cause distraction or discouragement, leading to procrastination. This can add further overwhelm or induce self-soothing behavior with sugary foods. At work, mundane tasks for which we are overqualified can make us feel bored or frustrated, leading us astray. And, as I mentioned in chapter 3, a common trigger I see with clients is the "stress creep" that goes unrecognized and untreated as the day progresses, derailing goal achievement.

Do you have unmet needs for comfort? Love? Fun? Spontaneity? Connection in a social activity? Perhaps you feel a need for organization and/or a sense of control? Do you crash and give up later in the day because you've denied yourself breaks from high-level thinking?

Identifying the cue will help you uncover what need the habit is satisfying. It's important not to *judge* that need once you can see it. Just accept it. Remember that self-compassion piece we practiced earlier? That's especially important here because we're dealing with Survival Bitch's needs.

The process of discovering the cue associated with any particular habit takes a thoughtful approach and considerable self-awareness, so give yourself as much time as you need to think through it. Your mindfulness practices will come in awfully handy here too.

Step Two: Simple Substitution with New Cue Planning

Once you've determined the underlying need driving your habit, the next step is to decide what new habit you want to replace it with. As you've learned, the trick here is to make sure that the new habit fulfills whatever need the old one was satisfying—that underlying need you discovered when you figured out what the trigger was for the old habit.

Coming back to the example of Betsy from the start of the chapter, the biggest cue we found for her ice cream habit was eating it at night when she felt lonely and in need of comfort and connection with loved ones. If you remember, the habit she chose to replace ice cream with at night was pampering herself in other ways, like giving herself a foot massage with nice-smelling lotion while she gabbed with friends or her mom on the phone. Comfort. Check! Feelings of connection. Check! This was a terrific substitution and turned out to be highly effective for Betsy.

Once you start implementing your replacement habit, it's important to repeat it over and over. Consistency is key. You'll find that this is *much* easier if you can tie the new action to an already-existing Repetitive Bitch routine (i.e., another existing habit that you want to keep). For instance, if you decide you are going to replace the habit of sleeping in with running every morning to better meet your need of stress management, then place your running shoes next to the cat treat container because you know Patrick is not letting you miss his treat time any morning soon. Or, if you want to get in the habit of writing in your new gratitude journal every morning, set it right next to your vitamins or the coffee maker. You get the idea. This technique is known as "habit pairing," and it works because the new habit gets wired in with the existing one—literally, wired into the same neural pathway that the first habit exists in within your brain. How's that for putting Repetitive Bitch's powers to good use?

Some prep work is almost always required until your new habit gets hardwired in. One of my favorite prep-work techniques is to use reminders while I'm still trying to wire in a new habit. This can basically be considered self-cueing your new habit. Thanks to modern technology, you can use apps on your devices for reminders timed to the minute, but I like to kick it old school and use sticky notes. I leave those suckers *everywhere*, writing down my goals and dreams, motivational quotes, and various quirky images and doodles—anything that will remind me to do the thing when and where I am supposed to when I'm trying to wire in a new habit.

Location is important here. If you want to start a new morning routine and every morning without fail you take the dog out, put the note by her leash. Remember, this works just as well for difficult mindset habit change too. Notes of "Don't rescue!" or "Weekends are sacred" can be helpful near the spot where you sit and chat on the phone or on your desk at work.

Variety also helps. If you're using sticky notes or some other too-hip-to-be-cool analog medium for your reminders, change up the color, design, and placement of your notes to self. If you don't, your brain will eventually start to filter them out as a normal part of your environment that doesn't require the spotlight of attention and "seeing." (I see *you*, though, Repetitive Bitch, you sly vixen. Respect.)

Timing is important too. Pick a time of the day or week when your stress is lower for goal-planning and/or larger executions (you want Charge Bitch *in* the building if at all possible!), blast some favorite tunes or a great podcast, and get it done. Block time in your schedule if necessary.

A big pitfall I see clients fall into is trying to wait until the end of the day to start new routines, and by then, they are often already feeling tired or stressed out. It's still doable to stick to a new routine at this point in your day if you get all that prep work we just talked about going consistently. By that point in your day, though, Charge Bitch has more or less tapped herself out, and the other Bitches like to grab control. When Survival Bitch is in charge, she's going to crave the comforts of old familiar routine, so unless the prep is completed and you have your reminders up, Repetitive Bitch will try to slide back in to run the show using the old habit you're trying to kick. That's why I use reminders that show me *why* I'm making the change. Remember, Survival Bitch needs to see what the reward looks like!

Step Three: Remove Old Triggers

Now, in order to keep Repetitive Bitch on board with your new habit, you've got to do your best to make the substitution habit appear easier than the old one you're giving up. Otherwise, Repetitive Bitch will keep insisting that sticking with the old routine is more "efficient." And you know what that means . . . she starts enabling Survival Bitch's pitch to stay on the couch with a bag of everything bagel chips and your latest Netflix binge while your laundry pile grows and grows.

One of the best ways to make a new habit easier is to make the old one *harder* to do by removing whatever triggers or cues are associated with the old habit. For instance, are you trying to give up coffee and replace it with tea? Don't just put that fancy tea collection sampler you picked up smack in the middle of your kitchen island. Get rid of or hide the coffee too!

The idea here is to remove the decisional choice and the need for willpower. This sets you up for much better odds of taking actions that align with your current desires versus falling back into Repetitive Bitch's old patterns.

Do you need to remove certain foods from the house that you know are not the best option for your current goals? If you must get dressed and drive to the store to get the Chunky Monkey ice cream you're craving, then you've already significantly lowered your chance of falling back into the habit you really want to stop. This is a much bigger deal than it may seem because even if you *do* choose to go get the ice cream, you made a *decision* and therefore weakened Repetitive Bitch's pernicious power of working on instant autopilot. Falling prey to that instant gratification with habits you're trying to break leaves you feeling that you didn't even have the *opportunity* to tap into Charge Bitch's long-term thinking desires and do differently.

It is helpful to change up routines attached to habits you're trying to break so that you're not receiving the same triggers or cues. Different people, places, and sights can help more than you'd think. One of my clients made a deal with herself about fast-food drive-through stops, as they were her Achilles heel. If she wasn't willing to get out of the car and go into the restaurant, then she decided it wasn't really a need, and she would forgo the treat. But if she wanted to go inside and get her order, then she felt it was a sign she was truly hungry, and she got her food without self-flagellation.

Another client gained weight when she took a work-from-home position. I asked her where she was doing her work. Can you guess? The kitchen table. Talk about a cue to eat! She said she seemed to be grazing all day while seated. Taking my advice to find an alternate place to work, she set up a cute space in her basement, started using a simple phone app that reminded her to drink water and take more steps, and purchased a reasonably priced standing desk. Losing weight didn't have to be about forcing herself to do something she didn't want to or adopting a grueling and unrealistic diet. These tweaks made a huge difference, not just in her weight, but in her energy and productivity for the day.

Often my clients find they really need to renegotiate how they engage with the people in their lives too; for instance, asking a friend if they would like to go for a walk or to a painting class instead of going out for their weekly drinks. Or perhaps they decide to ask family members to alternate the hosting of Sunday dinners instead of doing it at their place every week and starting the workweek off exhausted. Breaking old habits and replacing them with better ones ain't easy, but even small steps like these add up to huge wins.

Step 4: Directly Tie Your New Behavior to Rewards

The next step in the process of replacing an unwanted habit with a new and improved one is convincing your Bitches that the new desired behavior will be a rewarding one. We talked about this a little in the first step, but it's so important that it deserves a step of its own. The trick here is to associate your new habit with the reward you're going to get from it and to anchor the two together intrinsically in the brain. This step leverages the fact that our brains are wired to seek and notice reward opportunities and go after them.

For instance, if your goal is to meal prep more consistently to create a healthier dinner routine, maybe you decide, "Okay, I'll meal prep on Sunday. Then, Monday through Thursday in the evenings, I'll spend the extra time I'd usually spend cooking to read a couple of book chapters for the amazing new book club I joined." Another example would be, "For every week where I get up early five out of seven of those days and perform my stretches, I will book a massage for the following week."

Now, the key here is to not flake out on yourself. If you make yourself a reward promise associated with keeping a new habit, it's important to follow through. Rewards you offer yourself can be short term, external, and superficial in the beginning, until all the great benefits of the change completely unfold internally. After all, these temporary rewards are a stand-in for the long-term rewards that your brain will come to associate with the new habit.

Sometimes it can be a little while before you notice those long-term, lasting rewards from a new routine, such as clarity and improved mood with a healthier diet, a boost in confidence with regular workouts, or better mood regulation with consistent meditation. Until that time, be purposeful about liberally adding outside rewards. Eventually, you may find you don't need to rely on them as much. Many of my clients come to *want* to exercise because they have begun to associate it with a post-workout biochemical rush. The trigger or cue to exercise, in this case, eventually becomes that craving for and anticipation of the feel-good endorphins, epinephrine and endocannabinoids that were so satisfying in the past.

Be intentional! This technique may not seem like much. After all, you're really just making a deal with yourself. The thing is, it really works. And if for some reason it doesn't, add in an accountability partner (i.e., a supportive friend or a professional coach). This helps to alleviate any sense you may feel of trudging through the effort alone.

Embrace True Change

Now you have a better sense of how habits work and how your Inner Bitches play into the process. You're armed with a bunch of exercises, tools, and methods you can use to hack Repetitive Bitch's routines. Be forewarned that this doesn't mean you should try to make all the changes you're looking to make all at once! Start slow, one or two things at a time. Let those new patterns and routines sink in and take root before adding in something else new.

Once you can begin to see this process and the exercises I've introduced here with a curious and nonjudgmental mindset, *everything* changes. Finally, you can start to develop plans for substitutions that meet your needs and offer true rewards and benefits, only without the literal or proverbial hangover.

Experimentation is highly encouraged. If you're unsure about what need an old habit has been designed to meet, sometimes you have to make a best guess and give the solution a try. If you make false starts and are still unsatisfied, then at least you are learning about yourself. That time is never wasted. Eventually, you'll land upon the right tools and solutions to meet all your Inner Bitch needs.

Remember, you can't necessarily erase old habits, as they stay encoded in the brain, but you can replace them with your new "go-to" action. One day, you'll awaken to a new set of patterns that don't require extra thought or effort. Autopilot installs complete. Soon it begins to feel *weird* if you skip your new routines, and because they leave you feeling authentically satisfied and with an increase in self-respect, you'll find yourself never wanting to stop what—ironically—you never wanted to start.

I guarantee this attitude of "I can do it and I deserve it" will carry through to other areas of your life. And that's where you start to come into your full power—your Powerful Bitch superpowers.

CHAPTER SEVEN:

HOW TO EMBRACE CHANGE LIKE A POWERFUL BITCH

"When we deny our stories, they define us.
When we own our own stories,
we get to write a brave new ending."
— Brené Brown

Passing through Fire

This is the hard part. Big change does not come without some fear. Fear is only natural, given that evolution has primed us to view anything new or different with wariness. And an unfortunate reality is that, for many of us, fear and uncertainty can stop us from taking chances and making significant changes in our lives. Hopefully though, armed with the information in this book, lasting change actions will become more doable *and* less intimidating for you because you will understand the pitfalls to avoid and why they existed in the first place.

Trust me, you *do* possess the power to initiate practices that, when repeated enough, will create that permanent type of change you are seeking. Remember, this is you using intention to create routines that result in your own form of powerful change, change in something you value. As we discussed in chapter 2, that is self-directed neuroplasticity, the makings of a Powerful Bitch.

To illustrate how powerful our capacity for self-transformation is, I'm going to share a more extreme example of a problem a client of mine faced. Let me preface this story by saying that if you have a phobia as severe as the one I'm about to describe, I suggest that you consider working through it with a professional mental health specialist rather than trying to make this kind of change all on your own.

Norma was severely afraid of heights—and somehow she had tied this fear directly to elevators. The moment she walked into a building for a meeting or an appointment and saw that door with the column of little buttons next to it, she could feel her pulse and breathing start to speed up. Worst-case scenarios from horror movies started playing on a loop inside her head, accompanied by an all-too-familiar thought pattern: "If I get on that elevator, *I am going to die.*" Survival Bitch started screaming in her head using her outside voice. "No! No elevators! It's going to plummet to the basement, and I'll be a goner for sure."

So . . . she avoided elevators. She took the stairs instead. No big deal, right? Survival Bitch felt relieved and safe. The more Norma repeated this behavior, though, the more the thoughts and feelings that led to this behavioral pattern (along with the pattern itself) were reinforced. Every time she was faced with an elevator, Survival Bitch would vote loudly for avoiding it. After all, that's what Norma had done the last time, and she had survived.

Repetitive Bitch was also on board. She had the stair routine down pat. "We've habituated this as a work-around," she would say. "Come on. We're wasting time!"

But here's the thing: Sometimes it was just way too many stairs. We're talking ten or even twenty flights from time to time. And sometimes Norma either didn't have the time to take the long way up or didn't want to arrive at her destination sweaty and out of breath. Before she knew it, she found herself going out of her way to avoid important or fun things that happened on high floors.

She began to feel like avoiding elevators was limiting her life.

But that fear was real and *strong*. So what could she do to overcome it?

To begin, we decided together to see what might happen if Norma took a step back to acknowledge what was going on inside of her when she encountered an elevator. The next time she found herself face-to-face with one, she knew to pause and feel her heart racing, and she gave herself permission to breathe into that sensation. That was the first step.

Then she started in with her go-to mindfulness techniques. For Norma, this meant beginning with deep breathing for a count of five to calm down her nervous system. Regardless of what technique you prefer, engaging your mindful practice in the face of a fear like this lets you see the thoughts playing out in your mind and observe them, rather than standing directly under the flow. This reminded Norma that she was not her feelings and thoughts—that they were the product of her old stories and perceptions and their resulting chemical response.

After practicing these steps several times at the front of elevators (and then taking the stairs) and observing her thoughts, feelings, and sensations while deep breathing, her symptom management improved dramatically. Finally, one day Norma was ready to move on to the next step: She walked into the damn elevator and pressed the button for the fifteenth floor. And it started going up, up, up.

This was uncomfortable, but Norma was prepared. She used self-compassion to remind herself that all change is uncomfortable at first, until the new becomes routine. And she found that she was able to stand there in the elevator alongside her discomfort, labeling her fear stories as just that: stories.

She knew that she could tolerate this in the short term while she was learning to change her thoughts and behavior. After all, it's dang near impossible to convince Survival Bitch she's wrong about something (especially something like "We are gonna die!") until you can actually kindly but firmly show her evidence to the contrary.

After a few moments, the door chimed and opened and voilà! For the first time, Norma arrived at her annual physical appointment not huffing and puffing, not needing to wipe down with portable wipes. After repeating this exercise several times, she found that the "all-points alarms at elevators" conundrum finally slowed its roll. Once you get this far, the brain categorizes these alarm thoughts as "no longer useful" and stops prioritizing producing them. Eventually they stop autogenerating, or, at the very least, they show up with less frequency and intensity.

And just like that, you have changed your thoughts and behavior.

You have passed through fire and lived to tell the tale—or at least, that's how Survival Bitch will tell the story. We'll let her have this one. She's done a lot for us, after all.

Lean into Fear

Life is unpredictable. You never know when an opportunity for positive change is going to arrive on your doorstep. The key in being able to embrace change and ride the wave to more peace or purpose is twofold. First, you have to be able to recognize opportunities when they come along as just that: opportunities, not merely challenges or things to be overcome or borne white-knuckled and grit-toothed. Second, you have to be able to take action to seize opportunities for growth when you see them. This is a big part of why platform self-care matters. Taking care of yourself means you stay mentally and physically prepared to go for it.

Look, I get it. Boy, do I ever. For most of us, change is *scary*. And as we've learned, emotions like fear can easily distort our perception of events and the world around us—if we let them. But we don't have to let fear rob us of opportunities. In fact, fear actually becomes useful in becoming a Powerful Bitch, because it's often one of the first signs that a new opportunity has popped up. "Oh crap! That thing that I want is right over there! *Eeeee!*" Cue every worrisome thought you've ever had about failure, success, and everything in between when it comes to that thing—whether it's a career opportunity, a shot at a hoped-for relationship, or a chance to finally allow yourself to consider your own needs when you're accustomed to putting everyone else first all the time.

When you see an opportunity and don't take it, it's your confidence that suffers the most. If you can learn to lean into your fear instead of spinning out and freezing up, you can show yourself that you can do hard things. This then translates out into other life areas, no matter the domain in which you did the scary thing. For instance, if you found the courage to do your first 5K run, you might find you suddenly feel more able to take on a new role at work. In the long term, you find that you stop feeling stuck and helpless—because you are consistently gathering ample evidence that you *can* tackle challenges. Not only that, but a part of you begins to crave them!

None of this is easy, but here's the thing: Everything we've learned together up to this point about how the Inner Bitches both help and hinder us has primed you to be amazing at this. You have the tools you need to move forward. In your toolbox now are your increased self-knowledge (all of that Inner Bitch Neuroscience 101 stuff we've learned), strategies to rewire habits, mindfulness practices, and self-care and self-compassion skills. All the work you've done so far is about to culminate in choices you will make about your future for how you want to implement change. At first, these changes will feel uncomfortable and out of the norm. But, before you know it, you will have achieved a new normal that will change not only what you believe is possible in your life but what you come to understand as possible within you.

In this chapter, we're going to learn to embrace change by leaning into fear. We'll do this by learning to give language to our experiences and flipping the script on limiting mindsets. We'll also talk about how to navigate two of the big stumbling blocks to change I see clients grapple with day in and day out: getting so bogged down by worries that you get stuck in a chronic stress state and feeling unworthy of being loved for who you are instead of what you do for others.

Once you add these finishing touches to your Inner Bitch toolbox, you'll be able to greet new opportunities with optimism and excitement, leaning into any fear or discomfort and harnessing that energy to propel you forward instead of allowing it to take over and halt your progress.

You just have to give yourself a chance to see that *seeing is believing*. You can do it!

First up, let's take a long, hard look at what gets in the way of believing we have the power to transform our own lives.

Flip the Script on Limiting Mindsets

Okay, so we've established that, when you've decided something is scary, it is quite difficult to convince yourself otherwise using logic and facts alone. Survival Bitch needs to see evidence. The same goes for when she doesn't believe something will be rewarding or fun. When she has made up her mind that something is going to S-U-C-K, she digs in her heels just like she does when she's scared.

But if you show her proof, she can't help but get on board.

Flipping the script on limiting mindsets requires action. You have to show yourself that the script that is playing out inside of your head is often not reality, at least not the only possible one. For instance, if you struggle with feeling worthy of compliments, favors, and acts of service from others, it often doesn't help much to simply tally up all your great attributes and decide and declare your feelings of worthiness. Many of us have struggled in this arena, and the good news is that it is changeable. The slightly bad news is that, in the beginning, it will likely feel awkward or uncomfortable to simply accept generosity and kindness from others without equivocating in some way. To flip the script, watch for opportunities to receive with grace, deep breathe, and, instead of trying to use logic about why or how you have "earned it," say to yourself instead, "I'm really uncomfortable with receiving this, but I'm just going to live with that discomfort for now until this mindset changes because I want to live in authentic worthiness without the guilt and weirdness or the need to scramble and *pay it back or make up for it*."

Take a nibble at a time of limiting mindsets. To paraphrase a quote I heard once, "If you take away all the deficit ideas and stories you tell yourself, who are you? What is left? What would you do next with your magical life?"

Now that you know the mind creates thoughts it sees as "needed or useful," but that are sometimes holding you back from becoming the Powerful Bitch of your dreams, you can take action to do something about it. Going forward, we're going to employ some mindset tools to diminish the power and frequency of whatever unhelpful thoughts you're experiencing. We're also going to strengthen the ones that allow you to act in ways that align with your greatest hopes and wishes, and we're going to do all of this using the tenets of neuroplasticity.

Just like Norma did, the first step is to *pause*. Look at what is happening within yourself using your mindfulness practice to gain the authentic power of inner knowing and choice. What sensations do you feel in your body? When something seems intimidating, many of my clients identify tightness in the chest, shoulders, and neck or some of that notorious belly churning. On down days, they may describe general body aches and overwhelming fatigue. Let your body help you understand what's going on in your mind and spirit.

What we tend to do when we feel like this is to ignore it and soldier through—to keep moving and doing, avoiding the ickiness we feel rather than paying attention to it. The problem with this is A) it just waits until we become tired enough that we need to stop the hectic craziness or B) it gathers and grows into symptoms that, no matter how hard we try to distract, we just can't ignore. Since we can't get rid of what we feel by shoving it down or aside, we're going to try something different. We're going to simply offer whatever uncomfortable thing is present a gentle acknowledgment. Maybe that's "I feel sad" or "I feel angry or threatened or left out."

After we pause to acknowledge what's really happening, the second step is *owning* what's there. My favorite way to do this is something I like to call "surfing the wave," and the way it works is like this: We're going to ride the wave of our sensations of discomfort for between sixty and ninety seconds. During this time, allow for what you're feeling to morph, shift, and possibly even leave your body. This allows room to change not only the difficult feelings themselves, but, *much* more importantly, how you view your own capacity to deal with them.

If you can acknowledge what it is you're actually feeling and allow yourself to adjust to it by *pausing* and *owning it*, you'll find, over time, that whatever bodily reactions you have and whatever limiting mindsets you possess, they will loosen their grip on your life.

Name Your Experience

Another especially useful technique that helps you flip the script is to give creative language to your experience. While you're pausing and owning whatever uncomfortable thing is present, ask yourself this: What is the core description of these thoughts and emotions? *Name* what they are.

Whatever it is you find there, give it words. Nothing is off-limits. And you don't just have to think these words—it helps if you say them aloud or journal them. If you are not sure, guess. You will know in your bones when you get it right. Remember that there are no "wrong" feelings and that allowing yourself to feel what you feel and name it doesn't change who you are. It's just allowing whatever is there to be expressed.

This also works well with that harsh inner critic voice that leads us down a negative path now and then. While volunteering at Family Drug Court, I met a woman who referred to her nefarious internal voice as "Poison Ivy," which I thought was brilliant. Ivy told her things like "You might as well use—you are a loser. What difference does it make if you are clean? You have no life." Assigning this voice a name was a way for her to quickly identify the false messages that popped up, attempting to pull her toward using again. Another young lady I worked with had an inner critical voice that prevented her from being loud and proud of her business success . . . especially on social media. She named that one "Judge Judy."

It makes such an impact to assign a name to your inner critic. This creates familiarity and offers a quick way to catch your critic's unwanted presence before it wreaks too much havoc. It also allows for some much-needed detachment and sometimes the bonus of humor and levity.

In either case, naming your experience with a lens of self-compassion will pull knowledge up to the conscious and prevent your "me me me!" center from running amok unchecked beneath the surface. This will also help eliminate the foggy or murky feeling of not really knowing what's wrong—which makes us feel even *worse* than we already do—because now you've pinned the tail on the proverbial donkey and called it what it is.

Another reason why naming your experience helps so much is because, you guessed it, it summons Charge Bitch back into the building. Charge Bitch works well with language and words, rather than the messy unnamed sensations that accompany emotions—especially difficult ones. Once you give language to your experience, the situation can be grasped with more clarity. This allows you to *respond* based on your own authentic needs versus simply *reacting* to a stress response. The latter tends to keep us jumping from solution to solution without ever examining the root cause of the problem.

Let's look at an example. Imagine that you have a big job interview coming up. You're prepared, but you still feel nervous every time you think about it. So you try *not* to think about it, only it's a huge opportunity, so you can't help but think about it. But that nervous feeling keeps getting bigger and bigger.

If you don't put words to the feelings, they become this general unease, like an amorphous blob rattling around your mind, hijacking your body, creating a stress response. This response is prime feeding ground for fear to grow.

Instead of letting the amorphous blob run amok, what if you simply say aloud to yourself, "I feel intimidated by the idea of this interview. I'm afraid of being judged and rejected." You can then honor that nervousness and the normal need for acceptance and add a dash of self-compassion. Add something like, "It's okay that I feel like this. These things are a little scary. That's normal. What have I done that worked well to reduce my anxiousness in situations like this in the past? Hmmmm. Why don't I go for a walk? Then, when I feel calmer, I'll make a plan to manage the interview."

The amorphous blob pops like a balloon—it was nothing but air all along. Owning your feelings by naming them puts Charge Bitch back in the driver's seat, bringing her powers of planning and execution back online to deal with what is now an identified and easy-to-understand issue. Plus, there's an added bonus: using words to describe these emotional responses and thought patterns allows you to recognize them much faster in the future!

Now that you're prepared to own and name what you feel, let's talk about another common stumbling block to change: the never-ending cycle of worry so many of us are so darn good at getting ourselves into—and how to get the heck out of it.

Avoid the Worry Loop

Another pitfall I see many women falling into is what I call the worry loop, aka "worrying and scurrying."

I have a history of this myself. So many times, I convinced myself that if I future-worried like hell, it would be useful in preventing all-out tsunamis. It took me a long time to accept that I habitually worried about situations that never actually occurred and, if troubles did arise, my chronic worry state left me perpetually anxious and actually *less* equipped to deal with difficult issues effectively. As we've already learned, when we're looking to make big life decisions and take meaningful action toward reaching our goals, it takes a calm thinking state to keep Charge Bitch's superpowers in the building.

Many of my clients rationalize preparing for worst-case scenarios and trying to solve problems before they get a chance to get started. But, most of the time, all this "catastrophe pre-worry" does is keep them in a constant state of distress and disaster-prevention planning. This is the whack-a-mole game of stress (mis)management, if you will, unfortunately leaving no mind space for creativity and dreaming.

You know how this one goes. You worry about something for a while, "solve" it in your mind, feel temporary relief, and then, almost immediately, the next worry thought pulls into the brain station. Rinse, repeat. For many of us, this quickly turns into a disheartening self-fulfilling prophecy. Because these patterns lead to a chronic stress state, this reaffirms the idea that stress will be perpetual and therefore we'd better batten down the hatches and solve as many future looming disasters as we can, even if we have to do so in the middle of the night. (Trains and brains love to run at night.)

As you can see, most of the time, what we are worrying about is not as relevant as the *act* of worrying and our lack of confidence that we can self-regulate and handle difficulties as they arise. This is common, and, for many of us, it represents a very clear needs gap—a need for confidence that in the hard moments of life, *we can step up and be all right*. Just as painful and common is the need to change our perceptions regarding the availability (or apparent lack thereof) of support from friends and family when the load is too great to bear alone. We need to witness these patterns and their accompanying uncomfortable emotional responses with gentle awareness and intentionally disprove them rather than slipping down the rabbit hole of trying to use Charge Bitch's bandwidth to logically "solve" recurring thought bubbles of worry or isolation.

For example, imagine your kid is sick and you have to go to work. Charge Bitch may try to devise a plan, but she is a little shaky because Survival Bitch is feeling bad that her kid is suffering and is simultaneously feeling the pressure of being the "perfect" employee and never missing work. This unsettled state may trigger old habit thoughts of isolation. The internal dialogue that comes up may tell you, "Well, no sense in asking the hubby if he will stay home because I always have to deal with this kind of stuff on my own." You feel worse and call a friend, who agrees to take on the babysitting. Worry thoughts about being a bad mom, being unsupported by your husband, needing to quit, and needing a nanny perpetuate all day. After a large online purchase from a vitamin shop that sells concoctions guaranteed to prevent kiddo icks, you realize that the reality is that you called your friend to babysit before your husband even woke up.

So now that you are armed with overpriced vitamins, a nanny interview, and a draft of your resignation letter, the situation seems to be cognitively and practically "solved," but you know what? The next time a situation arises that triggers the same old thought patterns and beliefs, you will end up feeling the same sense of aloneness and that chronic need to prepare to handle everything on your own. You never gave yourself the opportunity to flip the script by asking your husband to help. As always, it's important to take time with yourself and engage your mindfulness practices. That's how you can uncover the real or perceived unmet emotional or physical needs that are triggering the response, instead of getting bogged down and spinning in the details of the events. Let's face it, the pain is not the event itself, but the story of isolation around it.

You can do this work. So many of us simply don't give ourselves enough credit. We laser focus on perceived flaws, and it negatively impacts our emotions and behaviors, blocking the opportunity for grand choice and great possibilities. It was only once I started to finally appreciate that I could begin to question some of these old beliefs and act in ways that were contrary to their messages that my whole life changed.

You Are Worthy

Perhaps the biggest limiting mindset I see women struggling with is the nagging undercurrent of unworthiness. As we discussed earlier, the difficulty in asking for help or "putting others out" is common. Even more detrimental is when this struggle prevents us from asking for what we deserve in significant areas like work or love, leaving us feeling stuck in unfulfilling partnerships or stagnant careers.

And here we are at a stalemate. The healthiest part of ourselves knows for certain that we are capable, lovable, and worthy, but another part is yelling loudly out of fear of things like humiliation, rejection, or loneliness.

Unfortunately, as long as you continue to not ask for the support, opportunities, and accolades you need (and deserve), this myth of your unworthiness will perpetuate. You may find yourself picking up some resentment from your one-sided relationships or your less-than-satisfying job. But in actuality, your false story of unworthiness stopped you from even making the ask or taking the chance and going for what you really want.

Change begins with viewing and labeling these false perceptions of unworthiness with self-compassion and then, *while* these old narratives are playing their off-key tune in the background, taking the chance with the brave new choice or inquiry. Please be patient with yourself in the temporary discomfort. You are "showing" yourself something big and important, and that is hard. Now that you have mindful self-compassion and stress-management tools, you'll find you are better able to sit with your unease, knowing it is going to pass. And before you know it, Survival Bitch will have "seen" enough proof that asking for what she wants and deserves often means she will receive it. The story has changed—and so have you.

An Expansive Future Awaits You

I hope that by now I have shown you that you have power to change the limiting beliefs you carry. I hope you see that you do indeed have agency in chipping away at mindset barriers by doing differently. We have covered the details of how your unhelpful-but-once-useful thought patterns were birthed and how they gained strength and automation over time. Your most powerful weapons against these patterns are mindfulness and self-compassion while observing your Inner Bitches in action. We can't always control the thoughts our brains generate, but, with practice, we can notice and control our response to them.

When we control our responses, that will in turn change the type of thoughts we produce in the future, because our brains will begin to see that old narratives are just no longer true or necessary. Backslides are normal at times, and we can all get off track, but, with practice, we can catch ourselves and *realign* sooner.

With practice, your brain learns it can receive impulses, thoughts, and cravings and, rather than employing old methods of avoiding, distracting, or jumping into the worry loop, you can acknowledge your thoughts kindly, label them with words, soothe your nervous system, and choose a new response. This new response, once repeated enough, will eventually become Repetitive Bitch's new autopilot—but it will be a realigned response that serves you well *now*, as a kick-ass Powerful Bitch.

Now is the time to go forward in change and create the same thought automation but with beliefs around patience, worthiness, confidence, and acceptance. You will do this *by acting as though it were so.*

Once you choose growth and change over stagnation, an endless realm of possibilities opens before you. Eventually you will achieve a new way of being. One of the most telling phrases I hear from clients when I ask them about old behavior patterns they used to have trouble with is "Oh, that? I just don't do that anymore." And then they smile, and so do I.

Repeating these mindset changes one by one removes old limitations and is powerfully transformative. In the next and final chapter, we'll explore what it looks like to put all of your new knowledge, tools, and skills into practice.

CHAPTER EIGHT:

THE POWERFUL BITCH REALIZED

"Life is either a daring adventure or nothing."
— Helen Keller

Peace and Purpose Reclaimed

Monique was ready to give up on the idea of a richer, more fulfilling life when she arrived at my office door for coaching. At sixty-two, she was single with no kids and was an office manager for a thriving dental practice. For years, she had thrown herself wholly into her work, staying late and working even on her days off to keep on top of everything. Outside of work, she didn't have much of a social life, having mostly lost touch with her old friends and distant relatives, and she had set aside formerly enjoyable hobbies and pastimes.

Every day, she would get up in the morning, go to work, and come home late. On her days off—if she didn't go into the office anyway—she'd hang out with her ex-boyfriend. After all, that's who she was used to having in her life, even though he regularly brought up the idea of their getting back together and that wasn't what she wanted at all.

When she arrived home late from work, her go-to source of comfort was pouring herself more than one bowl of sugary kids' cereal, sitting in her comfortable recliner, and watching TV. Growing up with her two younger brothers, that had been their ritual—eating cereal together and watching TV. All those years later, a bowl of sugary goodness drenched in cold milk took her right back to the feeling of hanging out with her brothers and what offered her child self a sense of bonding and belonging.

Only, now that she was a woman of middle age, Monique's staying-home-alone-and-eating-cereal habit was leading to self-described detrimental effects on both her body and mind. She had been putting on unwanted pounds and was experiencing fatigue, brain fog, and irritability. She had tried giving up her nightly cereal binges many times, but she found this much harder than she expected. It had become a habit she couldn't seem to kick. She also wanted to make more time for herself outside of work to do things like focus on her health, get more exercise, and return to crafting, but she was having a hard time letting go of all the extra work tasks she'd picked up over the years to keep herself busy—like planning extravagant events for the staff and leading work-sponsored charity drives.

When she first arrived in my office, Monique was frustrated, feeling stressed out and lonely. She knew she'd backed herself into a corner by focusing so much on work, but she also believed her successful career was the one thing she really had going for her, and she was afraid of losing that if she stopped giving it 200 percent. So we set to work together, looking at the underlying reasons why she had developed habits like staying late every day and working on her days off. And what we found was that, deep down, she didn't feel worthy of her top managerial position and was always scrambling to prove to others—and herself—that she deserved it. After that aha was understood and faced with compassion, we knew that, in order to rewrite this false script of "not good enough," we had to show her Survival Bitch that, while well-meaning and protective, her assumptions were wrong.

The first change she decided to implement was small: "I'm going to leave work on time two nights a week and go to the gym." It wasn't easy at first. But Monique knew she would have to sit with her feelings of discomfort because the only way to overcome them was to forge straight ahead through them. She started leaving work on time on Tuesdays and Thursdays and heading to the gym, where she'd warm up on the treadmill and then go to an evening yoga class. The more she did this, the more she found herself falling into her new routine.

As Monique continued going to the gym, something began to change. She'd proven to herself (and to Survival Bitch) that she could take well-earned personal time and not be judged by her coworkers and her boss as a "slacker" and that she could make positive change and stick to it. What's more, working out and taking better care of herself made her feel *good*. She came home from the gym feeling relaxed and calm—so good, in fact, that she decided to make another change.

The workouts were improving her energy and confidence, but Monique still felt lonely in the evenings and on weekends and wanted to expand her social circle. We discussed this without shame or recriminations and brainstormed ways for her to go about finding these vital connections. She'd always loved scrapbooking and hadn't done it for years. So, after a quick internet search, she decided that she'd leave work on time three nights a week now—two nights for the gym, and one to get together with a group of women she had found who liked to sit and do crafts together.

Creativity plus new friendships was just what she needed.

Empowered by these first few changes, Monique increasingly left work on time—though there were starts and stops at first. She didn't always follow through because "Old Monique" showed up now and again (as our former selves often do), saying, "This is what people expect. Gotta stay longer. Make yourself indispensable." Only now, Monique had the tools to recognize when this was happening and catch herself before she could completely fall back into old patterns. Gradually, she delegated some of the extra tasks she'd taken on, like managing celebrations for the staff and customers, and she finally let go of the reins on many of the day-to-day duties that her staff had actually been asking to learn. She fully embraced her new routine of leaving work on time every day.

From there, change began to snowball.

Monique stopped hanging out with her ex all the time and finally found the courage to tell him that, while she wanted to maintain a friendship, they were never going to get back together. Unless an emergency arose, she steered clear of the office on her day off, and she began to dip her toe into the scary world of dating.

But my favorite change of all was yet to come. Monique had outlived her brothers. One had died in a car accident when they were children, and the other had succumbed to lung disease in his fifties—both gone far too young. It was only natural that her habit of binge eating sugary cereal had such a strong pull. But now that she compassionately understood the need it was meeting, she openly sought to replace it.

You see, cereal munching was not the only thing they'd loved to do together when the three of them were kids. They'd also lived close to a park with a playground. They went there together after school and on the weekends, and Monique's favorite memory was one of pumping her legs on the swings as she attempted to touch the clouds with her toes.

So, she did something totally and unexpectedly wonderful. At sixty-four, after two years of working with me and after all of the other changes for the better she'd made in her life, Monique bought a full-on, hard-core, pressurized, treated wood swing set and had it placed in her front yard. No kids, no grandkids—that swing set was just for her. And when she got home from work at night, when she felt a little blue or lonely, she'd go outside and swing, look up at the stars, and talk to her brothers. She told me once that if she closed her eyes and listened closely, she could hear them laughing.

The Keys to the Queendom

The key to finding peace and purpose in our lives is to do what Monique managed to do: instead of letting her Inner Bitches run her life for her on auto-pilot, she lovingly but intentionally took back the reins using her most insightful and powerful self. She became a curious inner investigator, looking beneath the surface to openly view the needs that we all have, for confidence, comfort, creative expression, and human connection. And it turned out that one of the biggest things she needed is something we all tend to forget and forgo: the act of play as an adult.

For Monique, the need for play was filled by scrapbooking, card-making, novel yoga classes, and, of course, reacquainting herself with her love of swing sets of all varieties. She decided "to hell with what the neighbors might think"— she was going to do what brought her peace and joy. Honestly, what a freakin' rock star of a Powerful Bitch. To this day, I still love thinking about her on that swing.

But what is that going to look like for *you*? Maybe you already know, in which case, *awesome*. Or maybe you don't, in which case look forward to figuring that out—no, really, this is the fun part. Maybe play for you means time outside in nature, joining in make-believe games with the kids in your life, or picking up a creative hobby or sport you used to do or always wanted to try—whether that's playing backgammon, horseback riding, or rowing a kayak.

Be deeply curious and ask questions.

Who were you before the world's judgments took hold and changed who you wanted to be?

What gives you energy, joy, meaning, and purpose?

What could you plan that would come close to that waking up on Christmas morning feeling?

Who are you without the roles and titles of mom, wife, daughter, or how you earn a paycheck?

I want you to be able to walk into a room and, when someone asks you who you are, instead of explaining with titles, say, "I am obsessed with eighties music and I love to run in the rain. That's who I am."

Maybe what lights you up inside is playing with makeup and doing live video tutorials, or starting a book club, or laughing your butt off at local comedy shows with friends. Whatever it is, give yourself permission and time to explore it and make it a regular part of your life. Act like you do not need to worry about others' opinions—and eventually you won't.

Again, I would feel remiss if I didn't circle back to the painfully prevalent issue of unworthiness that many of us suffer with silently. *You are not alone.* As discussed earlier, lovingly understand that these stories were written with childlike understanding and long before you grew into the wonderful, amazing, kick-ass woman who is reading this today.

Finally, accept that it's going to be uncomfortable until it isn't. Change is hard. Acting as someone who deserves and is capable of great things takes patience and practice. Maintain your platform, use *all* things stress management, and keep a watchful eye for opportunities to flip those old unhelpful scripts. I promise the discomfort will lessen, until the once-scary or uncomfortable becomes commonplace and you begin to actively look for new hills to climb. My most powerful clients have, over time, become growth-edges seekers versus avoiders, much to their oh-so-happy surprise.

A Powerful Bitch Is a Self-Compassionate Bitch

Unless you are Thelma or Louise, this type of change cannot all be done in one fell swoop. I tell my clients to pick the easier challenges first. One client began by creating and enforcing privacy boundaries with her mother-in-law. Number one was "call before you come over." Another client never let her husband pack their three-year-old's lunch for preschool for fear of "judgment" from the teachers over its contents. She acknowledged this uncomfortable limiting fear, went against the old "you must keep doing it" directive, and allowed him to take this over. Once she had practice in this, she found pleasure in having the time to do her hair and makeup before work, which gave her a sense of preparedness in facing the day. The common denominator in these situations is that, despite the presence of old voices telling them that the potential new behavior would harm them in some way, each of these women leaned into their brief discomfort and made the best choices for them *now*. The old stories, once disproven, came up less and less. Self-compassion and intention equated to freedom from the old patterns that were making them feel stuck. You'll find this to be true for you too.

It's only fair to warn you that, of course, there will be times when you are completely overwhelmed and miss a step here or there or fall back into old patterns for a day or a week. That's okay. I tell my clients just to gently note the events where they may have failed to capture the opportunity in real time and to revisit the reaction in meditation to play out the way they would like it to go in the future. Assume the best of yourself and, next time the situation or a similar one arises, trust that you will be ready to make a choice aligned with your most Powerful Bitch needs.

Powerful Bitches United

It's also important to know that you don't have to walk this path of personal transformation on your own.

"Old" Shawna tried to do it on her own. Like most women I saw going through various difficult things, I didn't talk about it during all the years I felt stuck and helpless. None of the women I knew talked about it when things were hard, I think mostly out of fear or due to the perception we might be bothering people with our messy, sticky emotions. I look back on that now and see so much needless additional suffering. I wrote this book because I have tended to do things the hard way in my life, and I wanted to give women a guide so they may follow a less lonely and arduous path.

No more saying we're "fine" when we're not. No more living with unworthiness or shame or feeling futile in efforts to make lasting significant change. And no more trying to go it alone.

Find someone, whether it's a trusted friend or family member or a trained professional, to talk to about the things you're learning about yourself and what you need to become your most Powerful Bitch self. Find someone who will offer you support and encouragement along the way. Even better? Find someone else who wants to make similar changes in her life—or join a group of women to potentiate that power.

After all, Powerful Bitches *love* to support one another.

If you're looking to connect with others in your area, sites like MeetUp are a great way to look for like-minded people with similar interests in self-improvement (and just about anything else you might find intriguing).

For a more in-depth look into some of the topics discussed in this book, I highly recommend the works of Dr. Kristin Neff (self-compassion.org), Jon Kabat-Zinn (mindfulnesscds.com), and Eckhart Tolle (eckharttolle.com), as well as the wealth of articles at verywellmind.com.

If you're looking for a wellness coach to guide you along the journey, you can get in touch with me through my website at http://shawna-oliver.com/ or through LinkedIn https://www.linkedin.com/in/shawna-oliver-rn-nbc-hwc-b1a89b6b/ I offer both individual and group coaching. Many examples of my group coaching workshops can be found on my website and include such topics as impostor syndrome, dealing with stress, and goal setting and achieving.

The Future Is Powerful

While a Powerful Bitch might sound like someone who is coming in and knocking down doors, what she truly embodies is a full certainty and confidence in her intrinsic value and worth. She gives from a place of desire and embraces reciprocal and healthy relationships. She has given up the worry and scurry routine to remain present in her days and capture those beautiful opportunities in everyday living. She yearns to be with others in a way that brings about joy, deep connection, and a *whole* lotta laughter.

The Powerful Bitch understands that self-care makes her kinder. She knows that pushing herself to the point of physical and emotional pain will lessen her ability to offer empathy. So, she takes care of her needs without unhelpful "guilt" stories and leans into asking for support from others, bouncing back better to return the favor with authenticity and strength.

The Powerful Bitch also leans into discomfort with intention when she knows it will lead to growth and expand her possibilities. She may—just may—

come to thrive on it. She can sit with her discomfort when she sets out to make a change because she knows the feeling is only temporary and that she is strong enough to face it down on her road to becoming her powerful self.

Finally, the Powerful Bitch stands side by side with Survival Bitch, Repetitive Bitch, and Charge Bitch. She knows they all have their own superpowers and they have carried her to the place where she sits today. She knows they will still be there no matter what the future holds.

All of this is what I see for you—a future where you've forged yourself into a version that is ready to tackle challenges or adversity but also just as ready to soak up all the well-deserved good. You are prepared to go forth and find whatever brings you peace and a deep sense of purpose and connection.

I see the Powerful Bitch in you. And soon, you'll see it not only in yourself, but in others around you.

After all, it takes one to know one.

Made in the USA
Middletown, DE
02 May 2023